The ultimate rescue

The ultimate rescue

Christ's saving work on the cross

D. Eryl Davies

 EVANGELICAL PRESS

EVANGELICAL PRESS
12 Wooler Street, Darlington, Co. Durham, DL1 1RQ, England

© Evangelical Press 1995
First published 1995

British Library Cataloguing in Publication Data available

ISBN 0 85234 332 9

Printed and bound in Great Britain at the Bath Press, Avon.

To
Pastor John M. Davies,
my natural and spiritual brother,
also my colleague in the ministry of the gospel
of the Lord Jesus Christ

Contents

	Page
Preface	9
Introduction	11

Section I: The cross: the background

1.	Rescue	15
2.	God's plan	21
3.	Preparation	29
4.	Promises	37
5.	A special birth	46
6.	Qualifications	54
7.	Mission	63

Section II: The cross: a historical event

8.	A royal welcome	73
9.	The cup	80
10.	A court case	89
11.	The case continued	96
12.	Suffering, torture and crucifixion	105
13.	Parting words	113
14.	Dead and buried	122
15.	Alive again!	129

Section III: The cross: man's need

16. Disaster   139
17. Pollution   146
18. God   155
19. Sin   165
20. Guilty!   173
21. God — holy and angry   180
22. Danger   187

Section IV: The cross: God's answer

23. The cross   195
24. Sacrifice   200
25. Redemption: freed but at a price   206
26. Propitiation: God's wrath diverted by sacrifice   214
27. Justification: not guilty   221
28. The substitute   230
29. Reconciliation   237
30. The cross: specific and effective   244

Section V: The cross and you

31. The cross: salvation secured and applied   255
32. A glorious harvest   264
33. A personal challenge   269

Preface

I have wanted for some time to write a book on this central, biblical doctrine of the atonement. Now that the project is completed, I want to thank those who have helped and encouraged me. Mrs Chris Connor worked from my scribbled notes to put the manuscript on to disc and also revise it on several occasions; her help was invaluable. I am also indebted to my wife, who diligently and competently edited the page proofs immediately prior to publication. Due to the pressures of college work and also domestic circumstances, I failed to meet numerous deadlines for the completion of the manuscript but the directors and staff of Evangelical Press have been extremely patient with me and understanding.

I am thankful to say that, from the time of my conversion in college, I was taught the importance and significance of Christ's sacrificial work. The influences of the university Christian Union and the Theological Students' Fellowship were formative while, in terms of preaching the cross, two men helped me profoundly. One was the Rev. Vernon Higham, who is now serving as Pastor of Heath Evangelical Church, Cardiff, through whom I became a Christian. His burning passion always to set the person and work of the Lord Jesus before sinners in the clearest and most biblical way has

continued to challenge me. The second man was the late Dr D.
Martyn Lloyd-Jones, who through his teaching, preaching,
writings and friendship highlighted for me the glories as well
as the marvels and sufficiency of the cross. I am grateful to
God for these two men and others who have helped me to glory
in, and preach, 'Jesus Christ and him crucified' (1 Cor. 2:2).

May God bless this book for his own glory.

Eryl Davies
Evangelical Theological College of Wales
Bridgend
March 1995

Introduction

The theme of this book, the death of Jesus Christ, is approached from four different but related directions. Starting from the main biblical teaching and the model of a major rescue operation, the significance of the Lord's sacrificial death is first highlighted, set in context and illustrated.

The book then directs its focus on the historical events surrounding, and leading up to, the death of Christ. Jesus Christ was a real historical figure. His unique death actually happened, too. He was buried and three days later he was raised from the dead. Jesus Christ is alive! Here is a well-attested historical event of enormous significance.

We then change direction again in order to see the death of the Lord Jesus against the wider canvas of God's holy character and man's sin. Because of sin, our need of help is desperate and the danger facing us is real and awful. Without the sacrifice of the Lord Jesus, there is no hope of anyone being saved. No one else is able to rescue and reconcile sinners to the holy God.

In the last section of the book, the direction changes yet again. This is necessary because of the need to understand more of the Bible's teaching concerning the Lord's achievement on the cross. What did he do there? How does he save by his death? Some of the biblical concepts and categories such as sacrifice, substitution, propitiation, redemption, reconciliation and justification are then introduced in order to answer these questions and demonstrate the triumph of the Lord's death.

In the concluding section, my task is twofold. First of all, I want to show that Christ's sacrifice is effective and fruitful. He did not die in vain. Secondly, I remind you briefly of the personal challenge facing you in the light of the Lord's death. Are you a Christian? Have you received Jesus Christ as your personal Saviour? Or, if you are already a Christian, do you seek to please the Lord Jesus in your life? These are questions which need to be answered honestly and urgently.

One final word: the many illustrations in the book are used with a fourfold purpose — namely, to interest, retain attention, illustrate and also relate basic biblical principles to other areas of life. Like many people, I prefer to think and express myself in picture-language; my frequent use of illustrations is, therefore, important and deliberate.

Section I
The cross: the background

1.
Rescue

It happens every day. People are rescued from danger and imminent death. A father died saving his wife, three children and a baby-sitter from a fierce fire in their home in England. A part-time lifeguard risked death when he rescued a twenty-year-old woman who had been swept off the rocks in South Wales while trying to pull her dog out of the water. 'The sea was very cold and there was a heavy swell,' he remarked, 'but I managed to get her back to the rocks.' Although the woman was safe, the lifeguard was suddenly dragged under the water and it seemed that the exhausted rescuer would himself drown. However, some fishermen on the rocks acted quickly, holding out a rod for him and, when next he surfaced from under the water, they were able to pull him to safety.

Or let us take a different example. In October 1989 a powerful earthquake in San Francisco killed at least fifty-five people and injured another 300, as well as causing about six billion dollars' worth of property damage in the area. The earthquake, one of the most deadly in the United States since 1906, measured 6.9 on the Richter scale and the tremor lasted for fifteen seconds. An estimated 800 people were made homeless. Five days after the earthquake, doctors fought successfully to save the life of a man rescued from the rubble of a collapsed motorway. A rescuer spotted the injured man moving his hand in a car which had been almost flattened under concrete from a collapsed two-tier motorway in Oakland, across San Francisco Bay, after hope had been abandoned of finding anyone alive. The man had three broken ribs, a broken skull and a crushed leg, but survived.

Christ came on a rescue mission

It is this concept of rescue which underlines much of what the Bible says about the death of the Lord Jesus Christ. He died in order to rescue us. We were unable to rescue ourselves from the power and punishment of our own sin, but 'Christ died for the ungodly... God demonstrates his own love for us in this: While we were still sinners, Christ died for us' (Rom. 5:6,8). One Greek word for 'rescue' is used in Galatians 1:4 to describe the purpose of the Saviour's sacrifice on the cross: 'who gave himself for our sins to rescue us'. This term implies great danger as well as the inability of the people concerned to escape from the danger by their own efforts. On the cross, therefore, the Lord Jesus Christ achieved a special rescue operation and one which it was impossible for any human or angel to accomplish. The same idea of rescue occurs again in 1 Thessalonians 1:10: '... Jesus, who rescues us from the coming wrath'. Only believers are rescued from God's anger, but notice that it is the Lord Jesus *alone* who rescues us from this 'coming wrath'.

What a rescue mission involves

Rescue work is often difficult and extremely dangerous; it also involves preparation, courage and commitment. For example, the lifeguard referred to earlier stripped off most of his clothes before diving into the sea to rescue the young woman, and he almost drowned. Or think of the heavy, tedious work undertaken by the emergency services in rescuing the man from under the collapsed motorway in San Francisco.

There is one story which illustrates the point in a telling way. In August 1977, John Everingham, an Australian journalist working and living in Laos, was expelled by the Communist authorities after ten years of residence and work there. Sadly, he was compelled to leave behind his girlfriend, Keo, whom he loved deeply. Over the following ten months, John thought constantly of Keo and planned how he would rescue her. On 27 May 1978, when his preparations were complete, John Everingham set out on his mission. Fitted with masks, fins, an oxygen tank and two breathing devices, he plunged into the swollen Mekong River. He had a compass stuck to his face-mask because of the zero visibility under water and he battled hard against the river currents. At times he tried to crawl along the muddy river-bottom and at others he was tossed around helplessly in whirlpools. It was a difficult and dangerous mission. When he eventually surfaced he was still several hundred metres off shore and well past the spot where Keo was waiting with a fishing-pole and a child in order to avoid arousing suspicion.

Exhausted, John swam back to the Thai side and tried again but this time entered the river further upstream. 'I made it,' he exclaimed, 'and I crawled out on to the river bank. Keo had given up hope and was walking away so I yelled and then she saw me and ran and fell into my arms.' John had prepared well for the return because Keo was unable to swim. He put a slightly inflated life-vest around her neck and a breathing regulator in her mouth. With their faces at surface level and a quick-release strap binding them together, John pushed hard into the current in order to gain distance from the Laos side.

Eventually, they made it and Keo had been rescued. This exciting story has been popularized in a book and film.

There are a number of aspects of this story which help us to appreciate the Lord's rescue of sinners on the cross. In the next six chapters, we will look at such matters as planning, preparation and mission. But there is one point I want to underline before I close the chapter.

Love

All that John Everingham did in planning and achieving Keo's rescue was motivated by love. It was not duty, or even pity, which made John go to so much trouble in order to bring Keo out of her homeland; no, it was love. Essentially, John's story is one of romance and the lengths to which love will go in finding and rescuing a loved one.

How much more true is this of our Lord Jesus Christ in saving his people on the cross! He did it because he loved us. The Bible speaks of 'the Son of God who loved me and gave himself for me' (Gal. 2:20). Or again, we read in Ephesians 5:25: 'Christ loved the church and gave himself up for her.' The extent of those to whom Christ's sacrifice applies is deliberately emphasized here, namely, 'the church'. This is a reference to all whom the Father sovereignly chose to save, and it is for these specifically that the Lord Jesus died on the cross. 'To him,' wrote the apostle John in an attitude of worship, 'who loves us and has freed us from our sins by his blood...' (Rev. 1:5). The Lord Jesus completed a glorious but costly rescue mission. It was costly, for 'He poured out his life unto death,' and 'was numbered with the transgressors. For he bore the sin of many...' (Isa. 53:12). All this was done because of his love for us.

This point was underlined by a Christian teenager in an art class a few years ago. John was a promising artist who enjoyed drawing and painting. Near the end of a school term, his class were encouraged to paint any scene of their choice. For John, his mind was made up. He was going to paint the crucifixion scene. It was a difficult task but his aim was to depict the Lord Jesus Christ hanging on the cross with some of the people laughing at him. Several lessons were taken up with the project; eventually, there were some finishing touches to be made before showing the painting to the teacher. It was not a masterpiece in any sense but the teacher was impressed by the realism of the work. Examining the painting in more detail, he pointed out some weaknesses before drawing attention to one glaring omission. 'Where are the nails in the hands and feet holding Jesus to the cross?' he asked. 'You had better put them in.' John's response was unexpected. 'I know the nails should be there,' he replied, 'but I wanted to leave them out.' By this time the teacher was intrigued and wanted to know the reason. With some shyness, John explained, 'It was not the nails which held the Lord Jesus Christ to the cross but his love for us. Love kept him on the cross, not the nails.' And it is true. 'Christ loved the church and gave himself up for her' (Eph. 5:25). Katherine Kelly, the hymn-writer, asks:

Was it the nails, O Saviour,
That bound thee to the tree?
Nay, 'twas thine everlasting love,
Thy love for me, for me.

Another hymn-writer, Isaac Watts, depicts the desperate plight of sinners and also the Saviour's love in rescuing them on the cross:

Plunged in a gulf of deep despair
We wretched sinners lay,
Without one cheerful beam of hope,
Or spark of glimmering day.

With pitying eyes, the Prince of grace
Beheld our helpless grief;
He saw, and oh, amazing love!
He flew to our relief.

Down from the shining seats above,
With joyful haste he fled;
Entered the grave in mortal flesh,
And dwelt among the dead.

Oh! for this love, let rocks and hills
Their lasting silence break,
And all harmonious human tongues
The Saviour's praises speak!

A glorious and unique rescue, certainly! Remember, however, that love prompted and motivated it throughout.

2.
God's plan

John Everingham had planned for months how he would get his beloved Keo out of Laos. As we saw in the last chapter, the plan was a brilliant one, and it worked. In all kinds of ways, planning is an essential part of human life. A teenager plans, for example, which examination subjects to sit and what kind of career to aim for. Or it may be a wedding which is planned. The date, guests, clothes, the venue — a church or registry office — and the honeymoon all have to be planned in advance. The menu for a special meal is planned before the food is bought and prepared. Older couples like to plan their retirement. Where will they live? How will they spend their time? Then there is the architect who plans the specifications and design of a new house, or the sports team which plans the tactics it will adopt in the next competitive game or race. What about planning holidays? It can be fun, although problems can arise. Can we afford it? Which are the most convenient dates? Where shall we go? Are our friends or family free to come with us? All this involves planning.

Businessmen need to plan the manufacturing and market-ing of their goods. Politicians also plan carefully, both in the context of domestic and international affairs. The economy, taxes, law and order, education, health and defence are all matters which require in-depth planning.

On occasions, plans can be directed towards evil and cruel ends. An armed robbery of a bank is usually planned with meticulous care. Or think of the way in which the leaders of the Republic of China in the spring of 1990 planned how they would end the fifty-five-day struggle for democracy in Tianaamen Square, Beijing. On most of those days, over two million people converged on the square chanting their criticisms of the country's corruption. They demanded the democracy which students claimed that the late Hu Hu Yaobang, former Secretary General of the Communist Party who died on 15 April 1990, had promised. During the months of April and May 1990, the government leaders, in their private and forbidden city of Zhonganhai, planned their responses. Their cruel plan was implemented on the nights of 3 and 4 June. Thousands of troops arrived through the underground network of tunnels and bunkers under the city of Beijing. Several armies were also encamped around the city; they were moving to battle-readiness in response to commands issued from inside Zhonganhai. The result was the massacre and capture of many people in Tianaamen Square; it was a massacre which shocked the world.

What of Saddam Hussein of Iraq, who implemented his evil plan of killing tens of thousands of Kurds in recent years? Even prior to the Gulf War, 4,000 villagers were killed by chemical warfare and 3,839 towns and villages were destroyed, as well as 1,757 schools and 271 hospitals. All this cruelty was planned and deliberate. Hussein's invasion of Kuwait in early August 1990 was also planned, as was the Allied response and victory in subsequent months.

Planning is certainly a feature of human life. It should be no surprise to us, therefore, to learn from the Bible that God also makes plans. In fact, all that happens in the world is ultimately decided and planned by God, 'who works out everything in conformity with the purpose of his will' (Eph. 1:11). And God's plans were not made hurriedly, or in an emergency. Not at all. God planned all things before the world was created. The result is that all history is the unfolding of God's eternal plans or decrees.

God, not fate, is in control

This means that our lives are not abandoned to fate or chance. It is the living God, not fate, who plans our lives and controls the world we live in. Here is a compelling reason for avoiding horoscopes, fortune-telling, tarot cards and reading of palms or teacups. For it is God, not the 'stars', who controls our lives and decides our future. 'The Lord reigns' (Ps. 97:1), declares the Bible, and he alone is in charge of everyone and everything in the universe. That is what the pagan king of Babylon, Nebuchadnezzar, discovered many centuries ago. As the king boasted of his fabulous building projects and military success, God struck him down with a mental illness until this proud man acknowledged God's control of his empire. It worked! (Read Daniel chapter 4). A few months later, the king's sanity returned and he worshipped God, saying,

> All the peoples of the earth
> are regarded as nothing.
> He does as he pleases
> with the powers of heaven
> and the peoples of the earth.
> No one can hold back his hand
> or say to him: 'What have you done?'
>
> (Dan. 4:35).

Rather than pry into the future, we should trust God, believe the Bible and accept what God plans for our lives.

Another reason for avoiding all forms of fortune-telling is the absurdity of the astrology that underlies it. Think about it for a moment. Astrology is well over 2,000 years old, yet astrologers claim to be able to predict the future through observing the 'stars'. But our knowledge of the universe has improved radically, even in the last 400 years and particularly in recent decades. Many new planets have been discovered and their distances assessed more accurately.

The fact is that God, not fate, plans and governs the universe. Now, included in God's plans for the world is his rescue of sinners through the death of the Lord Jesus Christ. Each aspect of this glorious rescue is planned by God, including the one who rescues, the timing of the rescue, the people chosen to be rescued (see, for example, Eph. 1:4; 2 Thess. 2:13) and the way in which they are brought to trust in Jesus Christ. All these things, and much more, have been planned by God in detail.

The rescuer

Consider it briefly. The Lord Jesus Christ was chosen by God the Father to undertake the awesome work of rescue. This choice was made and the plan drawn up even before the world was created. Here is what the Bible says: 'He was chosen before the creation of the world' (1 Peter 1:20). The word translated 'chosen' (NIV) is also translated as 'destined', 'foreknown' and 'foreordained'. The use of the same word in places like Acts 2:23; Romans 8:29 and Romans 11:2, as well as in the context of 1 Peter 1:20, shows that the foreknowing was God's plan from eternity in deciding that Christ himself would come as our rescuer and die for our sins.

The timing

But not only is the rescuer himself chosen and planned, even the timing of his rescue mission is planned. One United States president praised the benefits of the US space programme and called for a manned landing on Mars within thirty years. 'Thirty years from now,' he declared, 'I believe man will stand on another planet. I believe that before Apollo celebrates the fiftieth anniversary of its landing on the moon [July 1969], the American flag should be planted on Mars.'

Men cannot always keep to their proposed schedules. However, God had his perfect timetable for sending the Lord Jesus to Planet Earth on his rescue mission. This is referred to in Galatians 4:4 (AV) as 'the fulness of time'. His arrival at Bethlehem was at the exact time planned by God the Father. Our Lord's ministry, his temptations, obedience, teaching and miracles were all exercised according to a detailed, divine plan. There was nothing haphazard about his thirty-three-year life on earth; nothing was left to chance.

The time of his death, therefore, was also planned. On several occasions, his enemies tried to capture and kill the Lord Jesus but they failed, 'because his time had not yet come' (John 7:30; 8:20). However, on the night before the crucifixion, Jesus Christ was able to say, 'The hour has come for the Son of Man to be glorified' (John 12:23). In other words, the time planned by God for his death had now arrived.

Immediately after the Last Supper with the disciples, the Lord Jesus declared, 'The Son of Man will go as it has been decreed' (Luke 22:22). He was conscious that all the events of that final week and their timing were decreed by his Father. Later in the week, after the Lord Jesus had been hanging on the cross for several hours, he shouted out, just moments before his death, the words, 'It is finished' (John 19:30). It was a message of victory. He had succeeded. God's glorious plan to save sinners had now been accomplished. All had gone according to plan. But that was not the end of the plan. On the third day, God the Father raised his Son from the dead. The plan was carried out perfectly and on time.

The rescued

Who are the people to be rescued by Jesus Christ? You may think the answer is obvious and the question, therefore, unnecessary. Only those who believe in the Lord Jesus. That is correct. However, the question remains: did Jesus Christ die for everyone in the world? Or did he die for a specific group of people? To put the question more bluntly, did the Lord Jesus only come to make it possible for everyone to be rescued, or did he come specifically to rescue those chosen to salvation by the Father? It is the latter which the Bible teaches. This will be explained in more detail later in the book, so it is sufficient here to discuss it briefly in the context of God's plan.

Just as the rescuer, the timing and nature of his mission were all planned by God, so those rescued by him come within God's eternal plan. He left nothing to chance. Salvation was not devised by men. From beginning to end, it is one glorious, divine plan. It is the Father who chose a vast number of people to be saved (Eph. 1:4; 2 Thess. 2:13). And this choice was made in eternity and depends solely on the Father's will. Nor does man have the last word with regard to becoming a Christian. Those chosen by the Father were also given to the Lord Jesus to care and die for (see John 17:2,6-12). That is why the apostle declares, 'Christ loved the church and gave himself up for her' (Eph. 5:25). And his sacrifice on behalf of the elect is not in vain. The divine plan involves sending the Holy Spirit to these individuals; they are changed inwardly, brought irresistibly to Christ and given grace to believe on the Lord (see Eph. 2:1-10). In this way, the rescue accomplished objectively by Jesus Christ on the cross for the elect is applied and made effectual in their personal lives by the Holy Spirit. It is for these that Christ died, and they are the ones who are rescued.

Our debt paid

This idea of a plan, a plan arising out of love and involving considerable cost, came home to me forcibly on one occasion. I had been away from my church in Bangor, North Wales, for a week helping in a Christian youth camp. A couple of hours after I arrived home on the Saturday, the church secretary called to see me. He was the bearer of unexpected but happy news. While I was away, the church members had decided to send us away as a family for a week's holiday at their expense. We could choose where to go. I was overwhelmed by the kindness and thoughtfulness of the church members, especially as this was intended as a family holiday to enable my wife and me to celebrate a wedding anniversary. The children were delighted, especially when they heard that our pet dog could go with us. Our church secretary had contacted hotels in various places but we opted for a small hotel in a beautiful part of North Wales just thirty-five miles from home. All the arrangements were made for us by the church secretary and we eventually received a letter of confirmation from the hotel. Needless to say, we enjoyed the week immensely. The hotel was comfortable, the food was excellent and we relaxed throughout the week. On the Thursday and Friday mornings of that week, I noticed the guests settling their accounts with the hotel proprietor. No one asked us for money. Although we had been told that the church had paid the hotel for us, there was a nagging doubt in my mind. The children asked, 'Dad, do we have to pay anything?' To make sure, I asked the proprietor whether we owed him any money. 'No,' he replied, 'it was all paid for you before you came. You owe nothing!'

At that moment, I caught a glimpse of the love of Christians and I felt humbled as well as grateful. But I could also see the cross in a new light. Just as the church had planned the holiday so carefully for us, I thought, so the triune God planned Calvary in such meticulous detail. And it was a costly plan. The church had paid for our holiday in a two-star hotel; we would not have been able to pay for it ourselves. Suddenly, the proprietor's words set my mind thinking about the cross. As a sinner, I could not pay to God the obedience I owed him but Jesus Christ actively obeyed the law of God in my place. In addition, the Lord Jesus suffered the punishment and death I deserved because of my sin. 'It was paid for you. You owe nothing.' That is God's message from Calvary when we believe on the Lord Jesus Christ.

Yes, Calvary was planned by God. We are going to see in later chapters, however, that this plan was glorious yet costly for the Lord Jesus.

3.
Preparation

Having planned a glorious rescue mission, God prepared for it in all kinds of ways. This is another exciting fact about the cross which the Bible teaches. You may remember John Everingham, who made detailed plans to rescue Keo from Laos. In addition to planning the rescue, Everingham also made the necessary preparations over a period of months. For example, he bought all the equipment required and he improved his own swimming and life-saving techniques before finally setting out on his planned rescue. So it was with God's plan of rescue; he prepared for it over a long period of time.

This fact struck me on my first trip to the Republic of Korea. My visit had been planned over many months. In fact, so many churches and colleges were involved that the organizer was kept busy for months beforehand and actually went to Korea ahead of me in order to ensure that all the preparations and arrangements were complete. During the weeks I was in Korea, almost everything went according to plan; my friend Jong Tae Lee had prepared my itinerary thoroughly and thoughtfully. I was grateful to him for all his preparatory work.

Waiting for my flight at Gatwick Airport in London also illustrated for me the importance of preparation. After security and customs clearance, I waited for an hour or so with nearly 400 people to board our plane for Seoul. Through the lounge

windows of Gate 33 in the South Terminal, I watched officials
and technicians checking the engine and the underside of the
aircraft. A lorry was standing alongside refuelling the aeroplane while a van arrived with food and drinks for the passengers and crew during the long flight. Inside the terminal
building lounge, the stewardesses in their smart Korean Air-
ways uniforms arrived and boarded the plane. I caught a
glimpse of the pilot and his crew, then, minutes later, the
airport officials called us forward to check our boarding
passes. At last, I was sitting comfortably in my seat aboard the
plane and I realized that a great deal of preparation had been
made for the flight. The departure was prompt and within fifty
minutes of take-off we were flying over Helsinki. Another
twenty-five minutes and we were starting the seven and a half
hours of flying across the former USSR, now renamed the
Commonwealth of Independent States. To avoid North Korea, the route then took us over Manchuria in China and across
the sea to Seoul. It had been a non-stop flight of thirteen hours,
which modern technology and excellent preparation had
made possible, and we were only ten minutes late in landing
at Seoul. The need for preparation, of course, is not confined
to flying; it is a normal and essential part of everyday life.

What I want to emphasize in this chapter and the two
following ones is that the triune God prepared well and over
a long period for the Lord's death on the cross. One aspect of
this divine preparation will be pinpointed briefly in this chapter, namely, the Old Testament animal sacrifices. In the next
two chapters we shall see further how God prepared through
prophecy and the virgin birth of the Lord Jesus Christ.

The Lamb of God

While John the Baptist was preaching one day, he saw the Lord
Jesus approaching. 'Look,' he excitedly told the people

around him, 'the Lamb of God, who takes away the sin of the world!' (John 1:29). The next day, John again pointed to Jesus, exclaiming, 'Look, the Lamb of God!' (John 1:36). In the temple at Jerusalem, a lamb was sacrificed each day — in fact, both morning and evening. The people knew they could not approach God or obtain forgiveness without sacrifice. There was no other way to God. John's words, then, about the Lord Jesus were full of significance. The Saviour who had been prophesied and also pictured in the animal sacrifices of the Old Testament was actually here in person. His rescue mission had now commenced. 'Look,' John announces, 'the Lamb of God, who takes away the sin of the world!' Each generation of Jews had longed for him to come. 'Here he is,' says John. 'He has come at last and he is the one who will rescue us from our sin.' There is now need to retrace our steps a little in order to see how God prepared for Christ's sacrifice in the Old Testament.

Animal sacrifices

Very early in history, God introduced ceremonies and sacrifices whereby his people could approach him and enjoy his favour. The sacrifices involved lambs, bulls, goats and, for the poor, even certain birds. What was the purpose of these sacrifices? They were the means by which God passed over the people's sins, temporarily covering them for a period of time until Christ came and died as our sacrifice for sin.

Before we examine this point further, there is need to pause and consider an objection some people may have. Would God really ask people to kill an animal or bird as part of worship? You may find the whole idea repulsive. Possibly, you are an animal lover yourself and shudder at the thought of people having to slay an animal victim in order to have fellowship with God. You may go further and say, 'Animal sacrifice is cruel and primitive.' Perhaps, like my family you have a pet dog and are a member of the Royal Society for the Prevention of Cruelty to Animals (RSPCA). This society, for example, opposes fox-hunting. Chasing a fox for hours across fields and rivers, then allowing a pack of dogs to savage the exhausted animal, is deemed cruel. The RSPCA campaigns in many other ways for animal welfare, such as halting the export of live horses from the United Kingdom to Europe, exposing the evils of poorly run puppy farms and the ill-treatment of livestock or attempting to reduce the trade in wild birds and seeking a ban on animal experimentation in the production of cosmetics. Posters used in some of these campaigns are realistic but shocking, such as piles of dead dogs and horses hung from meat hooks, or young calves locked inside narrow, dark veal crates for months, where they suffer considerable discomfort, until they are ready for slaughter.

Perhaps you are interested in the International Fund for Animal Welfare (IFAW). Because of the 1992 Olympic games held in Spain, the IFAW focused attention on the torture of animals in Spain, especially on social occasions. Such torture involved bull-fighting, stabbing and shooting darts into a half-starved, drugged-up bull, hacking away at chickens with a blunt sword, throwing rocks at tiny animals trapped in clay pots and ripping the heads off live birds!

The question, therefore, is a pressing one. Did God really require the killing of animals as part of religious worship in the Old Testament period? Well, the answer is yes, but God did not authorize brutality to animals. Nor did he want the animals to die in sporting events. Not at all. The purpose was religious; the killing was humane.

There were different kinds of animal sacrifices (see Leviticus chapters 1-7) which God introduced. From the time of Moses, these sacrifices were normally offered in the mobile tabernacle tent and, later, in the permanent temple built in Jerusalem. Very near to the entrance of the tabernacle you would find an altar made from wood but overlaid with brass. Here the priest was required to place the animal sacrifice before proceeding further to worship God. Each day here, morning and evening, an animal was sacrificed and then burnt while the blood of the sacrifice was sprinkled on the altar. Such animals had to be without defect for they served as substitutes for the people worshipping God.

Right inside the tabernacle, in a small but important room, was the Holy of Holies. A heavy curtain barred people from entering this special place. It was special because God's presence was symbolized there. Only one piece of furniture was in the room. This was the ark, a small chest, or box, with a cover of pure gold. At each end of the ark was a cherub made out of gold with its angelic wings open, thus picturing the presence and awesomeness of God. Inside the ark, two tablets of stone were kept, on which were written God's law, the Ten Commandments. Only once a year was the high priest allowed to enter this special room. This was on the Day of Atonement. On that day, the high priest took with him the blood from the animal sacrifice and sprinkled it seven times over the lid of the ark called the mercy-seat. In this way, the sins of the people were covered and atoned for (see Leviticus chapter 16). The animal sacrifices were extremely significant.

Another occasion when God required animals to be sacrificed was at the Passover. It was about 1400 BC and the Jews had been slaves in Egypt for 400 years. God eventually sent Moses to Pharaoh, the Egyptian king, to demand their release. On several occasions, the pagan king refused but after each refusal God inflicted a plague on the Egyptians. The very last plague was the killing of all first-born male children and animals belonging to the Egyptians. However, there was protection for the Jews if they sacrificed a lamb and sprinkled its blood outside their homes. Only the mark of the blood of the lamb kept these families safe from death (see Exodus chapter

12). Afterwards the Israelites were required to observe the Passover annually in commemoration of this deliverance.

The purpose of these sacrifices

I can imagine you feeling uncomfortable about the whole idea of sacrificing animals. What was the point of such sacrifices? Were they really necessary? How did the sacrifice of animals help people to worship God? These are the questions we must now answer.

To begin with, it is important for you to appreciate the significance of the term 'blood' as it is used in the Bible. While encouraging and bidding farewell to the church elders of Ephesus, the apostle Paul told them to 'Be shepherds of the church of God, which he bought with his own blood' (Acts 20:28). In fact, Paul uses the term 'blood' frequently: 'Since we have now been justified by his blood...' (Rom. 5:9); 'In him we have redemption through his blood' (Eph. 1:7); 'But now in Christ Jesus you who once were far away have been brought near through the blood of Christ' (Eph. 2:13). The same word is used several times in the letter to the Hebrews: 'But he entered the Most Holy Place once for all by his own blood' (Heb. 9:12); 'Since we have confidence to enter the Most Holy Place by the blood of Jesus...' (Heb. 10:19). Or consider the apostle Peter's declaration: 'You were redeemed ... with the precious blood of Christ, a lamb without blemish or defect' (1 Peter 1:18-19). Similarly, the apostle John affirms: 'The blood of Jesus, his Son, purifies us from every sin' (1 John 1:7). Later, the same apostle writes, 'To him who loves us and has freed us from our sins by his blood' (Rev. 1:5).

These are only a few of the many verses in the Bible which refer to Christ's blood rather than his death. Clearly the term 'blood' describes the sacrifice of the Lord Jesus in the light of the Old Testament sacrifices. This is important for it shows there is a basic continuity between the Old and New Testament periods. Salvation is the same in both, namely, through grace and faith. In the Bible, 'blood' refers to the 'life laid down in death'. Blood was proof that the death of the victim had taken place. Concerning the animal sacrifices, therefore, in the Old Testament, the animal was first killed and later its blood sprinkled on the altar as evidence it was dead.

But we need to repeat the question: why blood? One important answer is that God's anger needs to be turned away from the sinner. Because of his holy nature, which makes him hate sin, God must punish sin. This fact will be explained more fully in later chapters, but remember that God's anger towards our sin can only be averted when a substitute is punished and killed in our place; this is what Jesus Christ did for sinners on Calvary. Here is the significance of the words: 'Without the shedding of blood there is no forgiveness' (Heb. 9:22). The reason again is that 'The wages of sin is death' (Rom. 6:23). There can be no forgiveness of sin, therefore, apart from the shedding of blood.

Signposts and shadows

Another important fact must be stressed. No priest or animal sacrifice in the Old Testament could obtain forgiveness for sinners. Their purpose was more limited. Like signposts, these animal sacrifices pointed forward to the one great sacrifice of the Lord Jesus Christ at Calvary. The sacrifices were also like shadows of what was to come — namely, the death of Jesus Christ.

These animal sacrifices of bulls, goats and lambs have been likened to token-money. For example, a sterling £5 note carries the words: 'I promise to pay the bearer on demand the sum of Five Pounds,' and this is signed by the Chief Cashier on behalf of the Bank of England. The note is a promise to pay the money. Similarly, animal sacrifices are tokens and promises by God during the Old Testament period that the amount will be fully paid when the Lord Jesus died on the cross.

The apostle Paul declares that God held back his wrath against sin during the earlier centuries: 'In his forbearance he had left the sins committed beforehand unpunished' (Rom. 3:25). An alternative translation is, '... the remission of sins that are past' (AV). 'Remission' here means overlooking or passing over; the phrase, 'that are past', refers to the sins of the people in the Old Testament period, so it is those sins which God passed over in his 'forbearance'. Such sins were only punished and dealt with when Christ died and dealt finally with *all* sin. God's wrath against sin was fully expressed only at Calvary when the Son of God died as a substitute for sinners. To this one, perfect and sufficient sacrifice of the Lord Jesus, the animal sacrifices pointed forward and in it they found their meaning.

A preparation by God for Calvary — that is an important way of understanding the Old Testament animal sacrifices. They anticipated and found fulfilment and significance only in the Lord's sacrifice on the cross.

In the next two chapters, we shall consider two other ways in which God prepared for Calvary.

4.
Promises

It is said that promises are like piecrusts, made to be broken! Sadly, that is how many people regard their promises. Some time ago, the sadness resulting from broken promises was vividly illustrated for me.

Most weeks I used to visit a local authority home for children in care. Aged between six and fourteen years old, the children were there for several weeks or months in order to be assessed, protected and rehabilitated. Usually they were there through no fault of their own; broken homes, abusing and indifferent parents were the main reasons for these children going into care. No wonder the children had emotional and behavioural problems. However, they responded warmly to expressions of love and kindness. Arrangements were made for some of them to attend Sunday School, to visit our homes and even go on holiday to a Christian camp. Two incidents stand out for me.

On one occasion, a boy of nine spent the day with my family. He joined in well, played, laughed and ate as if he had no worries. Quite frequently throughout the day, however, he referred to his mother and her promise to visit him. She had not been in contact for several weeks but had promised to see him the following Thursday. He was excited and his hopes were raised. When I next saw him a few days later, he looked sad and withdrawn. 'Did you see your mother?' I asked quietly. After a tense silence, he replied, 'No, she did not turn up. She promised and I was expecting her.' He then walked away in the direction of his bedroom.

Another incident was equally distressing, although unexpected. I arranged for a twelve-year-old boy to go away on a Christian holiday camp for a week during the summer vacation. He was excited and looked forward immensely to the holiday. I assumed responsibility for taking him, with my family, to the camp nearly 200 miles away. It was while travelling to the camp that I learnt more about the boy's broken heart. We stopped several times on the journey in order to stretch our legs, have food and also give the dog a walk. The first stop was near a park in a small town only thirty miles away from our home. The sun was shining as we walked for a few minutes and played around the trees in the park. Suddenly, the boy pointed in the direction of some houses. 'Over there', he said, 'my father lives… It is the last house on the right. He keeps promising to write and call to see me but he never does.' I knew that his father was violent and a heavy drinker but I had no idea where he lived.

Then the boy asked me a question: 'Do you know where my mother lives?' 'No,' I replied. 'You will not believe it, but she lives about ten miles from the place where we are now going for a holiday. The social worker says she has promised to come and see me one afternoon while I am in the camp.' He felt sure she would visit him, especially as he had not seen her for many months. You can probably guess what happened. By the end of that holiday week the boy was shattered and depressed. His mother had not called to see him despite her promise. It was not easy consoling him on the return journey. He felt rejected. I learnt later that the mother, despite her promise, had not intended seeing her son. To be honest, I felt angry.

Not all promises, however, are broken. Far from it. A lot of people recognize the importance of honouring their promises. For example, I recall the many promises made by my parents to me and honoured over the years. They meant what they said. Their promises were reliable.

God's promises

Does it surprise you to learn that God has made promises to us in the Bible? Some of these promises given by God are also called prophecies. Prophecy means that God plans and also foretells what will happen in the future. However, the word is normally used in a much weaker sense in everyday conversation. For example, people sometimes prophesy or predict the result of a sporting event, a government election or medical surgery. They are not always right in their predictions and sometimes these are no more than guesswork.

God's promises and prophecies are very different. For one thing, God does not, and cannot, lie (Titus 1:2). He never deceives or tells an untruth. It really 'is impossible for God to lie' (Heb. 6:18). This is one reason why the Bible, the Word of God, can be trusted. There are no errors or lies in it. 'Your word is truth,' said the Lord Jesus (John 17:17). Neither does God change his mind or withdraw his promises. He is 'the Lord', who does 'not change' (Mal. 3:6). That is not all. No one but God has the power and ability to keep promises. There is nothing too hard for God to do; to put it positively, 'With God all things are possible' (Matt. 19:26; Luke 1:37). And not only does God know everything, he is in absolute control of people and events; history is his story! He does what he wants and nothing can stop him.

For these reasons alone, we need to take God's promises seriously. He means what he says. And he will do what he promises.

Prophecies of Christ's coming and work

Now I want you to notice that in addition to the animal sacrifices in the Old Testament period which we discussed in the last chapter, God also prepared for the rescue mission by Jesus Christ through giving promises; that is, he foretold, gradually but clearly, the coming of the Lord Jesus Christ. These predictions were given in prophecies recorded in the Old Testament Scripture. There are so many of these prophecies that I can only refer here to a few examples.

The very first prophecy appears at the beginning of the Bible, in fact, at the beginning of the history of mankind. And it was given in sad and tragic circumstances which are described for us in Genesis chapter 3. Later in this book we shall look in more detail at this tragic event. For the moment, however, we need to note that the first humans, Adam and Eve, had just sinned for the very first time against God. Before they were told of their punishment, God first spoke to the devil of the punishment he would receive for having tempted Adam and Eve. Surprisingly, it was to the devil that God spoke, although guardedly, about the coming of Jesus Christ: 'And I will put enmity between you and the woman, and between your offspring ["seed"] and hers...' (Gen. 3:15). The promise is deliberately veiled. The 'offspring', or 'seed', of the woman ultimately refers to Jesus Christ and implies he will become man. Our Lord's victory on the cross over sin and the devil is implicit in the promise, 'He will crush your head,' while his sufferings are referred to in the words, 'and you will strike his heel.' It is a glorious prophecy and brilliantly foretold.

Some centuries later, God gave promises and predictions to Abraham. Here is one of them: 'And through your offspring all nations on earth will be blessed' (Gen. 22:18; 12:3). This was repeated later to Jacob (Gen. 28:14). According to Galatians 3:16, this prediction found its fulfilment in Christ. Another prophecy was given to Jacob, Abraham's grandson, when he lay dying in his old age:

> The sceptre will not depart from Judah...
> until he comes to whom it belongs
>> and the obedience of the nations is his
>>>>> (Gen. 49:10).

Included in this prophecy is the fact that the small nation of Judah will continue in existence and with a king until Jesus Christ comes; then, people and nations worldwide will obey their Saviour-King. And it eventually happened just as God predicted.

Progressively, God revealed more and more details about the coming of the Lord Jesus Christ. Some 700 years before Christ's human birth, God promised that 'The virgin will be with child and will give birth to a son, and will call him Immanuel' (Isa. 7:14). Again the promise was kept when the virgin Mary conceived a child in a miraculous way; the one born to her, Jesus, was indeed Immanuel, God with us (Matt. 1:23).

In Isaiah 9:6-7, God gave another prophecy concerning Jesus:

> For to us a child is born,
>> to us a son is given,
>> and the government will be on his shoulders.
> And he will be called
>> Wonderful Counsellor, Mighty God,
>> Everlasting Father, Prince of Peace.
> Of the increase of his government and peace
>> there will be no end.
> He will reign on David's throne
>> and over his kingdom

establishing and upholding it
    with justice and righteousness
    from that time on and for ever.
The zeal of the Lord Almighty
    will acomplish this.

Notice how divine names are given to the promised King Jesus in these two verses.

Even more well known is a prophecy describing with stunning accuracy the sufferings of the Lord Jesus on the cross. Yes, 700 years before the event, it was foretold in detail by God (Isa. 52:13 - 53:12). Here are a few of the statements:

He was despised and rejected by men,
    a man of sorrows, and familiar with suffering...
But he was pierced for our transgressions,
    he was crushed for our iniquities...
    and by his wounds we are healed...
    he did not open his mouth...
He was assigned a grave with the wicked,
    and with the rich in his death,
though he had done no violence,
    nor was any deceit in his mouth...
he poured out his life unto death,
    and was numbered with the transgressors.
For he bore the sin of many,
    and made intercession for the transgressors'
                                        (Isa. 53:3,5,7,9,12).

And it happened exactly like that!

Nearly 200 years later, several promises were given by God through the prophet Jeremiah. One is recorded in chapter 23:5-6:

...I will raise up to David a righteous branch,
a King who will reign wisely
    and do what is just and right in the land.
In his days Judah will be saved
    and Israel will live in safety.
This is the name by which he will be called:
    The Lord our righteousness.

As you read these verses, you will see that the Messiah is foretold as a descendant of David who will be a king, a judge, a saviour and also God.

Even the exact location where the Lord Jesus would be born was prophesied by God several hundred years beforehand (Micah 5:2). The one to be born in Bethlehem would be a ruler achieving worldwide authority and success. No wonder there was expectancy in Israel at the time Jesus was born. For example, when King Herod heard that a group of wise men had arrived in Jerusalem from the East, he 'was disturbed'. He felt threatened. Immediately, he called for the religious specialists who knew all about the prophecies in the Old Testament Scripture. Herod asked them where the Christ was to be born. '"In Bethlehem in Judea," they replied, "for this is what the prophet has written:

"But you, Bethlehem, in the land of Judah,
    are by no means least among the rulers of Judah;
for out of you will come a ruler
    who will be the shepherd of my people Israel"'
                                        (Matt. 2:1-6; Micah 5:2).

Once again, the prophecy was fulfilled. God had kept his promise, as he always does.

Many other promises and prophecies could be cited but the point has been made. God prepared for the rescue mission by

Jesus Christ through giving prophecies. These prophecies and promises mostly related to the person of the Lord Jesus, the type of rescue he would achieve and the glorious blessings which would flow to the world as a consequence. There is no doubt about it. The Old Testament points to, and finds fulfilment in, Christ.

The fulfilment of Old Testament prophecies in Christ

This fact was emphasized by Jesus Christ himself. 'You diligently study the Scriptures,' the Lord Jesus told the religious leaders in Jerusalem before reminding them, 'These are the Scriptures that testify about me' (John 5:39). Later in the conversation he challenged them: 'If you believed Moses, you would believe me, for he wrote about me. But since you do not believe what he wrote, how are you going to believe what I say?' (John 5:46). A similar point was made earlier to Nathaniel by Philip: 'We have found the one Moses wrote about in the Law, and about whom the prophets also wrote — Jesus of Nazareth, the son of Joseph' (John 1:45).

After his resurrection, the Lord Jesus met with his disciples on several occasions. On one of them he met two disciples walking along the road to the village of Emmaus, which was situated about seven miles outside Jerusalem. They told him of their sadness and the reason for it. Jesus of Nazareth was dead and their hopes had been dashed. But they were also mystified. Some women had reported to them that Jesus was alive, and it did not make sense. At this point, the Lord Jesus rebuked them. 'How foolish you are,' he said, 'and how slow of heart to believe all that the prophets have spoken! Did not the Christ have to suffer these things and then enter his glory?' Now notice what the Lord did next: 'And beginning with Moses and all the Prophets, he explained to them what was said in all the Scriptures concerning himself' (Luke 24:25-27).

Some hours later, the Lord Jesus met with the disciples as a group. They were frightened for they thought at first he was a ghost. After reassuring them, he told them that 'Everything must be fulfilled that is written about me in the Law of Moses, the Prophets and the Psalms.' He went on to tell them, 'This is what is written: The Christ will suffer and rise from the dead on the third day' (Luke 24:44-46).

God had prepared well for Christ's rescue mission. Not only the animal sacrifices, but also the prophecies and promises were given by God in preparation for Christ's coming and were fulfilled in him. And our Lord was conscious of fulfilling these prophecies throughout his ministry.

In the next chapter, we turn to consider the birth of the Lord Jesus — another important preparation for the Lord's rescue work.

5.
A special birth

In the last two chapters, we discussed important ways in which God prepared for the rescue mission by Jesus Christ. We mentioned, in particular, the Old Testament sacrifices and prophecies. Now we are going to look at another essential preparation for the Lord's rescue work, namely, his unique birth at Bethlehem. Sometimes the word 'incarnation' is used to describe what happened at this point. According to the dictionary, 'incarnation' refers to the taking of human form by a divine being. And this is a reasonable definition. In other words, Jesus Christ is God the Son. Within the Trinity of divine persons, Jesus Christ the Son of God is co-equal and co-eternal with the Father and Holy Spirit. To put it another way, the Son of God is not inferior to either the Father or the Holy Spirit.

God became man

Now here is a remarkable fact. For the purpose of rescuing us, the Son of God was willing to leave his home in heaven. But that is not all. In addition to leaving heaven, he also assumed a human nature. This again was deliberate, preparatory and necessary. Only by becoming man could he identify himself with us and actually die instead of us. As God, he could not die. However, as the God-man he could die in his human nature. This is how the Bible puts it: 'Since the children have flesh and blood, he too shared in their humanity so that by his death he might destroy him who holds the power of death — that is, the devil — and free those who all their lives were held in slavery by their fear of death' (Heb. 2:14-15).

In other words, to rescue us he needed also to be one of us. The writer of the epistle to the Hebrews continues: 'For surely it is not angels he helps, but Abraham's descendants. For this reason he had to be made like his brothers in every way, in order ... that he might make atonement for the sins of the people' (Heb. 2:17).

Ponder this for a moment: God became man. That is what the incarnation involved. In a staggering way, the Creator became a baby. The infinitely rich one became poor for our sakes. And the King eternal became a servant. The incarnation is not only an incredible fact, but also a necessary preparation for the Lord's rescue work.

An illustration may be helpful at this point. Early in 1992, a British Army general, Peter Davies, became a plain 'Mr'. After serving in other senior posts in Germany and in the Royal College of Defence Studies in England, Peter Davies enjoyed his work as an army general and in command of the army in Wales. It was a job he held for nearly two years. Then he switched careers. From an army general he became the chief executive of the Royal Society for the Prevention of Cruelty to Animals (RSPCA). Unlike nearly all other senior officers leaving the military for a civilian job, he lost his rank. And he did not miss it. 'I was asked about this by the chairman of the RSPCA Council at my interview,' he said. 'Was I prepared to drop my rank because I was dealing with a non-military organization? I replied that I had no inhibitions whatsoever.

Those who wish to call me "General" will do so — I'm still a colonel of the King's Regiment and I continue as Colonel Commandant of the Royal Signals... But within the RSPCA, I am "Mr Davies".'

The illustration has its limitations but it points, although feebly, to what the Son of God did in his incarnation. He was given a crucial job to do. Long before the world was created, the Father, Son and Holy Spirit agreed among themselves that the Son should save us by dying on the cross for our sins (1 Peter 1:20). To achieve this, he needed to be God but also man. Just as Peter Davies retained his military rank yet was plain Mr Davies to many, so the Lord Jesus remained God after his incarnation, yet most people imagined he was just an ordinary person. Some saw him only as the carpenter's son; they were oblivious of his deity and power.

Some questions need to be raised here. How did the Lord Jesus Christ, as God, become man? What was involved? And when did it happen? Well, this special person required a special birth. That is the significance of the first Christmas when God's Son, Jesus Christ, was born in Bethlehem 2,000 years ago. Let us think about this special birth for a moment.

The virgin birth

One day, God sent an angel to a young lady named Mary who lived in the city of Nazareth. Naturally, the woman was terrified on seeing the angel. 'Do not be afraid, Mary,' the angel said reassuringly, 'you have found favour with God' (Luke 1:30). But the next words spoken by the angel shocked her: 'You will be with child and give birth to a son.' Why should Mary be shocked? After all, it is natural for a woman to become pregnant. Yes, that is true. Nevertheless, there are facts concerning this pregnancy and birth which make it unique. Here is one important fact: Mary was still a virgin.

Although engaged to be married, she had not indulged in pre-marital sex nor did she cohabit with her fiancé. Mary really was a virgin and she could honestly say to the angel, 'I know not a man' (Luke 1:34, AV). She was telling the truth. No wonder she was in a state of shock. A virgin was to conceive and bear a son without sexual intercourse with a man and without help from modern medical science such as *in vitro* fertilization (IVF) or artificial insemination. No wonder Mary asked the question, 'How will this be ... since I am a virgin?' (Luke 1:34). She was told that her child would be conceived in a miraculous way by the power of God: 'The Holy Spirit will come upon you, and the power of the Most High will over-shadow you. So the holy one to be born will be called the Son of God' (Luke 1:35). The production of the sperm and then its penetration of the egg from Mary's ovary would be supernatural, not natural. Even the condition and development of the foetus in Mary's womb was under the direct control of the Holy Spirit. In such a way, the whole process of conception and birth was superintended by God so that the foetus was also protected from miscarriage and physical defects.

How the Holy Spirit did this work, we are not told. The details are withheld from us; the action of God is described only in a general and veiled manner. All that the angel tells Mary is that the Holy Spirit 'will come upon you' (Luke 1:35). In case Mary still found it difficult to believe that such a miracle would take place in her own womb, the angel re-minded her, 'For nothing is impossible with God' (Luke 1:37).

A unique birth

This special birth at least implies that Jesus Christ is a special person. Mary was told, for example, that she must give the name 'Jesus' to the child. Her future husband, Joseph, was given the same directive. The name 'Jesus' means saviour;

that is, 'He will save his people from their sins' (Matt. 1:21). In this respect, the Lord Jesus is unique, for he alone is able to save sinners.

But how special is Jesus himself? Is he only a great man, a famous religious leader, or even an angel? By way of reply, notice how the angel describes the Lord Jesus as 'the Son of the Most High', who 'will be great' and 'reign ... for ever' (Luke 1:32-33). He will also be called 'the Son of God' (Luke 1:35). Once again he is distinguished from others; he alone is the eternal Son of God.

Many times during his ministry on earth, he emphasized that he had come down from heaven (e.g. John 6:38). 'I am from above,' he told the unbelieving Jews (John 8:23). He did not begin to exist at the time of his birth. In fact, he claimed, 'Before Abraham was, I am' (John 8:58, AV). Abraham had died centuries earlier but Jesus continues to exist as the timeless 'I am'. Again, while praying for his people, he speaks of the glory which he enjoyed with the Father, 'before the world was' (John 17:5, AV).

No wonder that Mary was astonished when the angel told her that one so great would be born to her. By means of this special birth, the Word would be made flesh (John 1:14) and the King of the universe would become a servant. He who had made the universe, placing the sun, moon and stars in their position, would soon be a baby resting in Mary's arms. The high and lofty God who inhabits eternity was now to be restricted as a child in the stable. In this baby, however, the fulness of the Deity was to dwell in bodily form (Col. 2:9).

A thrilling story

Despite her astonishment, Mary responded in faith and obedience. "'I am the Lord's servant," Mary answered. "May it be to me as you have said"' (Luke 1:38). About nine months later, she gave birth to the child, just as God had said. At the time she was in Bethlehem, which was crowded with people. They had all returned to their home town at the direction of the Roman authorities in order to participate in the official census. Mary was there with her fiancé. Unfortunately, all the available accommodation had been taken, so Mary had no choice but to give birth to her baby in a stable.

Confirmation that her newborn son was someone special came to her within hours of the birth. A group of shepherds working in the fields nearby arrived to see the baby. Their story was a thrilling one. During the night as they cared for their sheep in the fields outside the town, they saw an angel and a brilliant light shining all around them. Naturally, they were petrified. 'Do not be afraid,' the angel told them. 'I bring you good news of great joy that will be for all the people. Today in the town of David a Saviour has been born to you; he is Christ the Lord. This will be a sign to you: You will find a baby wrapped in cloths and lying in a manger' (Luke 2:10-12). Immediately they went to Bethlehem and eventually found this special baby with his mother in a stable. They were excited and thankful. Finding it impossible to keep quiet concerning what they had heard and seen, 'They spread the word concerning what had been told them about this child' (Luke 2:17). Clearly, the startling fact of the incarnation had gripped these shepherds.

This was also true of a young missionary in the mid-twentieth century. Geoffrey Bull went as a missionary to Tibet in 1947. Within months of his arrival in Tibet, the Communists took control of the country. Eventually, in 1950, Geoffrey Bull was arrested and remained a prisoner for three years. He records an incident which occurred soon after his arrest in the autumn of 1950 and which helped him to appreciate even more what it meant for the Son of God to assume and restrict himself within our human nature. Because Bull was a Christian and also a Westerner, the Communists regarded him as a subversive and an imperialist. Moved several times after his arrest, he was kept for a period in a tiny cell in a remote prison on the Tibetan-Chinese border. It was a dirty, dark cell which he described as a small box. In fact, the cell was so small that he could only walk four steps in any direction and there was hardly enough space in which to stand upright. He hated the cell, with its filth and restrictions, but there was no escape. One day he began to think about the incarnation of the Lord Jesus Christ. As a baby in Bethlehem, Jesus Christ was confined in a way that no one else has ever known. In that small baby dwelt the fulness of Deity bodily. Here was an incomparable restriction. 'Think of His eyes,' writes Bull, 'accustomed to observe the earth from end to end... Yet as they open to His mother's face they have not focused yet... Ponder His hands. Moon and stars knew the touch of His fingers. All are His fashioning, yet Mary waits as any mother does for the little curl of her baby's finger about her own. Remember His feet. He it is who "rides upon the heavens by His name Jah," yet, as He lies sleeping in the manger, He must be turned in the hay. He who moves all things cannot move Himself... Recall His mighty words... Speechless He lies, quite unable, even in a word, to speak His need.'[1]

Here was a restriction unparalleled in human experience and one which the Son of God voluntarily accepted. Here was the body God had prepared for his Son. Couched and restricted within that baby in the stable was Deity, the one who is not contained in all the universe. This is how Charles Wesley describes the fact of the incarnation:

Our God contracted to a span
Incomprehensibly made man.

He laid his glory by,
He wrapped him in our clay;
Unmarked by human eye,
The latent Godhead lay;
Infant of days he here became,
And bore the mild Immanuel's name.

In another hymn, Charles Wesley again highlights the
wonder of the incarnation:

Christ, by highest heaven adored,
Christ, the everlasting Lord,
Late in time behold him come,
Offspring of a virgin's womb.
Veiled in flesh the Godhead see!
Hail the incarnate Deity!
Pleased as man with men to dwell,
Jesus, our Immanuel.

To rescue us the Lord Jesus needed to be made man. Here,
then, is another essential preparation for our Lord's mission.
In the next chapter, we shall look briefly at his qualifications.
There is no doubt about it: he was well qualified to rescue us.

1. Geoffrey Bull, *God Holds the Key,* Hodder & Stoughton, 1959, p.26.

6.
Qualifications

My dictionary tells me that the word 'qualification' refers to that which makes a person suitable and competent to do a specific job. Clearly, qualifications are important. For many jobs they are essential. And that is right, too. A medical doctor needs to 'qualify' through years of college study and hospital training before he can treat patients competently. Similarly, teachers need to obtain a degree and give evidence of teaching ability before obtaining a teaching post. For myself, I would have refused to board the aeroplane for Korea if the pilot and crew had not been trained and qualified. Currently, I teach in a college and help to train preachers and missionaries. Recently, I asked a few of my students about their qualifications for the secular work they did before entering our college.

Chris Tennant used to work for oil companies as a diver. He worked on a small oilfield near Bombay then on larger ones in the Persian Gulf. His last job was saturation diving, involving inspecting the welds of joints of oil platforms in the North Sea off Aberdeen in Scotland. What were his qualifications? He enjoyed swimming and had diving skills. In addition, he had served in the Royal Marines. But further training was necessary. Chris had to have an aptitude test and two separate twelve-week commercial diving courses. After this, he had a series of inspection courses with ultrasonics and photography video. A medical was compulsory and this was required every twelve months. Only after all this was he qualified to work as a diver for oil companies. His work involved deep diving in a diving bell for eight hours at a time.

Tony Dattani is an electrician. He, too, needed qualifications. Tony had a day-release each week to attend college and eventually obtained his City and Guilds in Electrical Engineering. For just over three years in his apprenticeship, he worked alongside qualified electricians. After his fourth year, Tony worked mostly on his own. It was hard work, too.

What qualifications are needed to be a speech therapist? Well, consider the training of Anna Myerscough. She studied full-time for a four-year degree course in speech therapy at Sheffield University. The course involved studying subjects like linguistics, psychology, speech and language pathology, anatomy, physiology, neurology and ENT. There were weekly placements, too, as well as a block placement at a head-injury unit. At the end of all this arduous training, Anna was qualified and able to work as a speech therapist.

Qualifications — yes, they are important and even essential. However, there are some people who only pretend to have the necessary qualifications for a job. A bogus medical doctor, for example, with no medical qualifications, treated and counselled thousands of unsuspecting patients for more than thirty years in the north of England; some time ago he was prosecuted in a Leeds court. Muhammed Saeed was 'living a lie' when he diagnosed complaints and wrote out prescriptions at his Bradford surgery, the court was told. The prosecuting lawyer said that the masquerade began when Mr Saeed copied details of a genuine Dr Muhammed Saeed's graduation from King Edward Medical School at the University of Punjab in Lahore. He then submitted these details to the General Medical Council on arriving in Britain from Pakistan in 1961 and after that he was 'qualified'! The real Dr Saeed left Pakistan for the first time in his life to give evidence at the trial.

Christ's qualifications for his rescue mission

How does this matter of qualifications relate to Jesus Christ? As we have seen, the Bible clearly teaches that he was appointed to rescue people from their sins. It was the most important and difficult task ever entrusted to anyone. What, then, were his qualifications? Was he the best person for the job? Or,was he an impostor like the bogus medical doctor in England? These are important questions which need to be answered before proceeding further.

The point needs to be underlined again: the qualifications of the Lord Jesus Christ are impeccable. He is outstandingly qualified to undertake this rescue work. No one else even approximates to him. He alone is qualified to save us. His claims are certainly not bogus. Sometimes in my own work I have to show my Curriculum Vitae (CV) to professional educators. The CV lists my qualifications and work experience. By looking at this CV, people can see whether I am qualified for certain responsibilities. And what we are actually doing now is looking at our Lord's CV and qualifications. They are most impressive. There is not a CV to compare with it anywhere in the world.

He is God

To begin with, the Lord Jesus Christ is God. There is no greater qualification for his rescue mission than this. Remember that in order to save us, the Lord first had to be without sin himself. As a divine person, Christ was without sin; unlike humans, he did not inherit the pollution and guilt of Adam's sin.

Again, his rescue mission was a huge task. For one thing, our Lord was not rescuing a small group of people. In fact, he was rescuing all God's elect in history from all generations and countries. It would be impossible for us even to number such a vast crowd of people, never mind rescue them. But the task was enormous for other reasons, too. The punishment due to us because of our sin had to be borne fully by Christ in his sufferings and death. That was unbearable at times even for the Son of God. While his sufferings were concentrated within a brief time-scale, yet only as God could he have absorbed such intense punishment and, at the same time, given to his sufferings and death a rich, infinite value. Also, only Jesus Christ as God could overcome a powerful, evil angel like Satan.

What superb qualifications! Jesus Christ is himself God and also without personal sin. But you may still have a nagging doubt in your mind: 'Is he really God? How can I be sure of the fact?' Perhaps you are aware of bogus claims made by leaders of other religions and cults.

Think, for example, of Joseph Smith (1805-1844), who founded the Mormons, or to give them their official name, the Church of Jesus Christ of Latter-Day Saints. He claims to have received the Book of Mormon from God as a fuller revelation of the gospel. But Smith was psychic; he was confused as a child and later misled by visions. Eventually, he claimed to have been led by an angel to the Book of Mormon, which was written on gold plates in an ancient Egyptian language. He is supposed to have translated it into English by means of two crystals. The whole story was a fraud. To begin with, scholars deny the existence of this ancient hieroglyphic. Nor is there any evidence that the gold plates ever existed. No one else other than Smith claims to have seen them and the plates disappeared rather conveniently.

Or think of Ron Hubbard's Scientology group. Even Hubbard's eldest son, Ronald E. de Wolf, who helped him establish the group in 1952, became thoroughly disillusioned with his father and his claims. Hubbard suffered increasingly from severe paranoia, delusion and ill-health.

What of Transcendental Meditation (TM) and its guru, Mahesh Yogi? It has been popular in the West since the 1960s

when the Beatles and then the Rolling Stones and other young-
sters explored its message and techniques. Even the Beatles
soon became disillusioned with the guru's claim to be 'a path
to God' and 'the only way to salvation and success in life'.

There is no doubt about it. Whether it is Joseph Smith, Ron
Hubbard, Mahesh Yogi, Mohammed or Confucius, their
claims are bogus. They are not what they claim to be.

Evidence that Christ is really God

The question, therefore, is pertinent. What about the claims of
Jesus Christ? Is he really God the Son?

Well, there is compelling evidence. For example, the Lord
Jesus performed many miracles, and these miracles were
astonishing demonstrations of power. He subdued a violent
storm on the lake, healed the sick and even raised people from
the dead. In fact, Lazarus, one of those he raised, had been dead
for four days and his funeral had taken place! No mere man or
angel could have worked such miracles.

The Lord's teaching was also distinctive and unique. 'No
one ever spoke the way this man does' (John 7:46) was a
common reaction of the people. The crowds 'were amazed at
his teaching, because he taught them as one who had authority'
(Mark 1:22; cf. Matt. 7:28-29; 13:54). Being God the Son and
'in the bosom of the Father' (John 1:18, AV), the Lord Jesus
Christ alone is qualified to teach and explain God to us. That
is why his teaching was so authoritative.

Remember, too, that our Lord's claims were proven in a
more remarkable way again. Referring to his body, he told the
Jews early in his ministry, 'Destroy this temple, and I will raise
it again in three days' (John 2:19-22). Here he claimed that he
would rise from the dead on the third day after his death. He
repeated the claim at regular intervals. At the halfway stage of
his ministry, he told his disciples that 'He must be killed and

on the third day be raised to life' (Matt. 16:21). Only days before his crucifixion, he gave the same prediction, but this time in even more detail: 'He will be turned over to the Gentiles. They will mock him, insult him, spit on him, flog him and kill him. On the third day he will rise again' (Luke 18:32-33). These were not empty claims either. It happened just as he had claimed. On the third day after his crucifixion, he was raised to life and many hundreds of people saw and heard him. He 'was declared with power to be the Son of God, by his resurrection from the dead' (Rom. 1:4). The ultimate evidence that Jesus Christ is the Son of God is his historical, physical resurrection from the dead.

We have digressed a little, so let me remind you where we have reached in looking at our Lord's qualifications. Two points have been made, namely, Christ is God and also without sin. Then, in order to illustrate that the claims of Jesus Christ are genuine, not bogus, I drew your attention to some compelling evidence from his miracles, teaching and resurrection.

He is man

Now we must move on and consider his qualifications as a man. As we saw earlier, it is a paradox. Jesus Christ was both God and man at the same time. And it was necessary for him to be man, too. As our representative and substitute, he needed to identify himself with us and he did that in his incarnation. 'For this reason he had to be made like his brothers in every way' (Heb. 2:17). Also, as a man, he 'has been tempted in every way, just as we are — yet was without sin' (Heb. 4:15). Supremely, however, he needed to become man in order to die physically on the cross for the punishment of our sins. Why? Because in his divine nature, he could not die. Here is how the Bible describes what God the Son did:

Who, being in very nature God,
      did not consider equality with God something to be
            grasped,
but made himself nothing,
      taking the very nature of a servant,
      being made in human likeness.
And being found in appearance as a man,
      he humbled himself
      and became obedient to death — even death on a
            cross!

                                                      (Phil. 2:6-8).

He was called by God

To conclude this chapter, three further points need to be made. The first is this: our Saviour was appointed and called by God the Father to undertake this rescue work. Even the Old Testament priests needed to be called by God to their work. 'No one takes this honour upon himself; he must be called by God, just as Aaron was' (Heb. 5:4). This still holds true for church pastors and missionaries today. They need to give evidence that God has called them. 'So Christ also,' the Bible adds, 'did not take upon himself the glory of becoming a high priest. But God said to him, "You are my Son; today I have become your Father." And he says in another place, "You are a priest for ever, in the order of Melchizedek"' (Heb. 5:5-6). Make sure you grasp the point for it is important. No one else has been called by God to rescue sinners. Uncompromisingly, the Bible announces, 'Salvation is found in no one else, for there is no other name under heaven given to men by which we must be saved ' (Acts 4:12).

He was equipped for the task

In addition to being called by God the Father to rescue sinners, Jesus Christ was also equipped in his human nature to do the work. This is part of the significance of his baptism, recorded in the Gospels. John the Baptist had been busy baptizing people in the River Jordan. To John's amazement, the Lord Jesus presented himself for baptism. After all, Jesus was not a sinner like other people and, therefore, he had no personal need to repent or be baptized. Understandably then, 'John tried to deter him, saying, "I need to be baptized by you and do you come to me?"' (Matt. 3:14). In reply, the Lord acknowledged the rightness of John's response but insisted, 'Let it be so now; it is proper for us to do this to fulfil all righteousness' (Matt. 3:15). The words are profound. He has partly in mind his own identification with the people. He is also ready in baptism to reaffirm his willingness to rescue sinners by his sacrificial death. His baptism, therefore, is deeply significant. Only after hearing this reply did John agree to baptize Jesus Christ.

I want to draw your attention to two important events which accompanied our Lord's baptism. The first was when the Lord Jesus stepped out of the water after his baptism and, suddenly, 'Heaven was opened' (Matt. 3:16) and 'The Holy Spirit descended on him in bodily form like a dove' (Luke 3:22). What is important here is that the Lord Jesus was being equipped by the Holy Spirit in his human nature to commence his public ministry and also complete his unique rescue mission.

The second important event associated with Jesus' baptism was the announcement from heaven: 'You are my Son, whom I love; with you I am well pleased.' This was the Father's voice. And the words express a unique, loving relationship between the Father and the Son. They also show that the Father approved fully the mission of the Son. In fact, we see in this baptism the Holy Trinity co-operating in our rescue. The Holy Spirit now strengthens and directs the Son throughout his ministry. God the Father announces his pleasure in the Son and his rescue mission. God the Son stands ready to commence his public ministry and, later, to die on a cross in Jerusalem for those chosen by the Father; he is now incarnate, the God-man, Jesus, the Christ.

Scripture is fulfilled

About six weeks after his baptism, the Lord Jesus returned to his home town of Nazareth. On the Sabbath, he went to the service in the synagogue. During the service, he read in public from the scroll of Isaiah the prophet these words:

> The Spirit of the Lord is on me,
>   because he has anointed me
>   to preach good news to the poor.
> He has sent me to proclaim freedom for the prisoners
>   and recovery of sight for the blind,
> to release the oppressed,
>   to proclaim the year of the Lord's favour
>
> (Luke 4:18-19).

After such a service, the normal routine was for the reader to roll up the scroll after reading, hand it to an attendant and then sit down. From a sitting position, he would then speak and explain the verses he had read. That was the procedure the Lord Jesus followed, too (Luke 4:20). The atmosphere was tense. There was great expectation. Everyone kept on staring at Jesus Christ. Then he spoke. However, his words were brief but unexpected. 'Today,' he said, 'this scripture is fulfilled in your hearing' (Luke 4:21). The long-promised one was now present. Perfectly qualified, he had embarked on his rescue mission. In the next chapter, we shall notice the Lord's awareness of his mission.

7.
Mission

There was no doubt about the mission of John Everingham. Only one thing mattered to him. That was the rescue of the woman he loved. There are, of course, different types of missions which people undertake for a variety of reasons.

Some of the men, for example, involved in destroying Hiroshima in a fraction of a second with the atomic bomb in 1945 returned forty-five years later, but this time on a mission of peace. On the morning of 6 August 1945, Charles Sweeney was a twenty-five-year-old American Air Force major and deputy to Colonel Paul Tibbets, commander of the 509 Composite Bomb Group specially formed for the atomic missions. Tibbets was the pilot of the *Enola Gay*, the B29 bomber which dropped the A-bomb on Hiroshima. It was a mission of destruction and death. Over 200,000 people were killed and twice this number were seriously injured in Hiroshima itself as an immediate, direct result of this atomic bomb. On this mission, Sweeney piloted the B29 that dropped scientific instruments to measure the bomb's radiation effects. Two days later, he commanded the bomber which dropped a second atomic bomb on Nagasaki, killing another 100,000 and injuring twice that number.

After forty-five years, Sweeney and four other crew members went on a different mission to Japan. Their mission was to take money to the orphans of Hiroshima and Nagasaki based in the Hokai-no-Sone home. This was one of the first buildings to open after the devastation. For over forty years, this home has sheltered hundreds of orphans, some of whose parents have died from the continuing effects of radiation. When the former crew members met the children, there were tears on both sides. After sending monetary gifts each year to the orphanage, Charles Sweeney explained, 'I finally decided I would like to see the children. So I asked some of my buddies on the mission to join me on a very different mission of goodwill.' Richard Nelson, who had been radio operator on the *Enola Gay*, admitted he had been reluctant to go on the peace mission but seeing the children, he added, 'all makes it worthwhile'.

Amanda Lawton went on a very different kind of mission. She went to Tanzania in an attempt to protect an endangered forest. As part of an Anglo-Tanzanian research expedition, Amanda spent three months camping in Mikumi National Park, surveying and mapping out the different ecological zones of the East African forest. Inland, the Miombo woodland is increasingly threatened by deforestation. The Tanzanian government invited a group of British students, including Amanda, to make an inventory of all the species and plants in the forest so that they could be better protected — a worthwhile mission, indeed.

Christ's mission

Appointed, planned, qualified and prepared — all this is true of Jesus Christ in relation to his rescue mission. What, then, was his mission? Certainly not one of destruction. Nor was it a mission of mere preservation or surveying. His task was to save those chosen by God the Father. What will be illustrated in this chapter is the Lord's own awareness of, and commitment to, this mission.

One fact stands out: his sufferings and death are central in all that the Lord Jesus says about his mission. Without his death as a substitute for us, his mission would not be accomplished. It is not surprising to find, therefore, that our Lord gradually gives more details concerning this mission as he approaches the cross.

A question about fasting

Quite early in his ministry, the Lord Jesus answered a question about fasting; it was specific and even pointed. The question was prompted because some people observed that both the Pharisees and the disciples of John were fasting. What they could not understand was why the Lord's disciples did not also fast (Mark 2:18).

In reply, Jesus Christ uses the picture of a wedding: 'How can the guests of the bridegroom fast while he is with them? They cannot, so long as they have him with them.' Here the Lord hints that he is a special person, unlike John or the Pharisees. While such a person is with them, his disciples have no need to fast. It is a privileged time for them. They cannot fast while they have such a glorious person with them.

However, warns the Lord Jesus, it will not always be like that: 'But the time will come when the bridegroom will be taken from them, and on that day they will fast' (Mark 2:20). Our Lord is conscious of his mission. There is a hint at least that a violent death awaited him, thus affecting this relationship with the disciples.

The sign of Jonah

On another occasion, it was not a question, but rather a request, which prompted the Lord to refer even more specifically to his mission, death and resurrection. But it was a tense situation. There was confrontation, too. The reason was that the religious leaders rejected the teaching and claims of the Lord Jesus. That was not all. His miracles were attributed by them to Beelzebub, the prince of demons (Matt. 12:24). This was slander. They had to be answered. The Lord Jesus Christ, therefore, warned them severely; that their slander was ridiculous (vv. 25-27), illogical (vv. 28-30), unforgivable (vv. 31-32) and only expressed their own evil natures (vv. 33-37). Imagine it! It was some of these people who made the request to the Lord Jesus: 'Teacher, we want to see a miraculous sign from you' (v. 38). Since they had rejected the proofs already provided concerning his claims, this request was deceitful and hypocritical.

They were refused the kind of sign they wanted, namely, something unusual and sensational. However, the Lord says, they would be given 'the sign of the prophet Jonah'. 'For as Jonah was three days and three nights in the belly of a huge fish, so the Son of Man will be three days and three nights in the heart of the earth' (vv. 39-40). The reference here to his mission and its accomplishment could not be clearer although some of the details are withheld.

His sufferings foretold to his disciples

Cæsarea Philippi was situated in the south-west region of Syria, although it is now occupied by Israel. Philip, a regional ruler, had enlarged the city, making it more attractive and modern. After the ambitious building programme was completed, he named the city in honour of Cæsar Augustus. It was

into this district that Jesus Christ came with his disciples
during the halfway stage of his public ministry. His main
reason for choosing this attractive area was to obtain privacy
and quietness. One or two significant things happened here.
First, there was Peter's remarkable confession concerning the
Lord: 'You are the Christ, the Son of the living God' (Matt.
16:16). This was followed by the Lord's teaching concerning
the building of his church (vv. 17-20). For the purpose of our
present study, verse 21 is especially relevant: 'From that time
on Jesus began to explain to his disciples that he must go to
Jerusalem and suffer many things at the hands of the elders,
chief priests and teachers of the law, and that he must be killed
and on the third day be raised to life.'

Notice how detailed the prediction is. There will be suffering. He will be killed. The religious leaders are involved. He
knows also that he will be 'raised to life' on the third day.

But Peter did not like what he heard. In fact, 'Peter took him
aside and began to rebuke him. "Never, Lord!" he said. "This
shall never happen to you!"' (Matt. 16:22). The rebuke from
Peter, however, was interrupted by Jesus: 'Get behind me,
Satan! You are a stumbling-block to me; you do not have in
mind the things of God, but the things of men' (Matt.16: 23).
He resists the temptation through Peter to be diverted from his
mission.

A week or so later, when Jesus Christ was walking down
from the mountain after his transfiguration, he made three
more brief references to his mission. 'Don't tell anyone what
you have seen,' he warned the disciples, 'until the Son of Man
has been raised from the dead' (Matt. 17:9). Minutes later, he
added, 'The Son of Man is going to suffer at their hands' (Matt.
17:12). After a couple of days, when they reached Galilee, the
Lord repeated these details: 'The Son of Man is going to be
betrayed into the hands of men. They will kill him, and on the
third day he will be raised to life' (Matt. 17:22-23).

His mission was clear, and he was conscious of it. He knew that it necessitated suffering and death. Many other examples could be cited to illustrate the Lord's awareness of his mission. However, I am confining myself to two contrasting examples in the rest of the chapter.

His distress

Calvary was not far away. But how did the Lord Jesus himself feel about it? Luke 12:49-50 is helpful in telling us more about the Lord's attitude and the distress he felt. 'I have come to bring fire on the earth,' he said. 'Fire' here refers to God's punishment of sin and describes his main purpose for coming into the world. The Lord continues, 'And how I wish it were already kindled!' The language and the longing here are similar to those of a woman who wants her labour pains to start so that the birth will be hastened.

His anguish is related to what is going to happen to him on the cross so he continues, 'But I have a baptism to undergo...' Again, it is figurative and colourful language. 'Baptism' points to the distress and pain into which he will be plunged. He is going to be overwhelmed by agony and desolation. Such was his mission. It was not an easy one at all. In fact, he declares, 'How distressed I am until it is completed!' There are no complaints here — none at all. Nor do the words express self-pity. What he is doing is sharing his innermost emotions and feelings as he reflects on the agony and humiliation ahead of him.

There were good reasons for such feelings on the part of Jesus Christ. He had great responsibilities. For one thing, the Father had entrusted the elect to his care; for these he must die as their sin-bearer. Extensive physical suffering was also involved. Even worse, there would be unimaginable spiritual suffering and desolation as the Father punished him in the place of sinners. 'My God, My God,' he would soon cry from the cross, 'why have you forsaken me?' (Matt. 27:46). Was he distressed? Certainly. However, he was determined to complete his rescue mission whatever the cost to himself.

The parable of the vineyard

The second example illustrating the Lord's consciousness of his mission is different. Actually, it is a parable he related and it is recorded in Mark 12:1-11 (cf. Matt. 21:33-46; Luke 20:9-19). The story is straightforward. It concerns a farmer who owned a vineyard and then leased it to some tenants. The contract involved the farmer having a percentage of the annual harvest. Some months later, the farmer's servant was sent to collect his rightful share of the fruit but he was seized, beaten and then sent away empty-handed by the tenants. Another servant was sent by the farmer but he was also treated shamefully. A third servant was actually killed by the tenants. Other servants were sent and they, too, were either beaten or killed by the tenants. The climax of the story is that the farmer's son was eventually sent but even he was beaten and killed. Now the farmer had no alternative but to execute the wicked tenants and lease the vineyard to others.

The application was obvious and 'They knew he had spoken the parable against them' (Mark 12:12). Certainly, the story's punchline is dramatic. To the surprise of his hearers, the Lord Jesus quoted, at the end of the story, words from Psalm 118:22-23:

The stone the builders rejected
    has become the capstone;
the Lord has done this,
    and it is marvellous in our eyes.

Jesus Christ was 'the stone' rejected by the Jewish leaders and people. Despite his being the Son of God, they would demand his crucifixion. All this was known to the Lord Jesus. He was aware of his mission; its details were familiar to him. In love, he moved forward to complete his glorious rescue mission. Was he successful? Yes, of course. The stone rejected by the builders 'has become the capstone'. In other words, the one crucified would rise triumphantly from the dead on the third day. Next, however, we will look in more detail at his sufferings and the events of that last week.

Section II
The cross: a historical event

8.
A royal welcome

All roads led to Jerusalem. During three separate weeks each year this was especially true, for many thousands of Jews made their way to the city from all directions of the country and even from the remotest parts of the Roman Empire. They were intent on celebrating one or other of the three annual Jewish religious festivals. Each festival lasted for seven days. On these occasions, the temple services would be crowded with eager worshippers. People thronged the streets. At times, the chatter, laughter and singing must have been deafening. Shopkeepers did a brisk trade. Houses and hotels were filled to capacity, although in one of the festivals the people were expected to live in booths made out of tree-branches. There was considerable joy in the city. Excitement was in the air.

Excitement and tension

Perhaps there was more excitement than usual on this occasion. The explanation was apparent to most of the people in Jerusalem at the time. Unusual things had been happening during the previous weeks and months in the country. For example, many astonishing healings had taken place. Even a dead man, Lazarus, had been brought back to life. The person responsible for all these miracles was Jesus Christ. Before the festival of the Passover began, therefore, the people 'kept looking for Jesus, and as they stood in the temple area they asked one another, "What do you think? Isn't he coming to the Feast at all?"' (John 11:56). There was plenty to talk about: 'Who is this Jesus?' 'How can he perform such powerful miracles?' Rumours were circulating, too, concerning the whereabouts and intentions of Jesus.

Actually, Jesus was not far from Jerusalem at the time. He was less than two miles from the city, having walked from Jericho to Bethany. He had probably arrived in Bethany just before sunset on the Friday and stayed there over the Saturday, the Jewish Sabbath, with friends. On the Saturday evening a supper was given in his honour in the house of 'Simon the leper' (Mark 14:3-9); it was here that Mary poured an expensive perfume over the feet of Jesus (John 12:1-3). Judas Iscariot resented Mary's expression of love, objecting that the perfume should rather have been sold and the money given to the poor. Bluntly, the Bible exposes his motive: 'He did not say this because he cared about the poor but because he was a thief; as keeper of the money bag, he used to help himself to what was put into it' (John 12:6).

Already, however, the religious leaders were plotting the arrest and death of the Lord Jesus (John 11:49-53). The people were given orders to tell the authorities if they knew where he was. There were also plans to kill Lazarus, 'For on account of him many of the Jews were going over to Jesus and putting their faith in him' (12:11). The situation was indeed tense. For Jesus himself, crucifixion and death were now imminent.

A donkey

It was a Sunday morning and, suddenly, it happened. The crowds in Jerusalem heard that Jesus Christ would soon be arriving. Unknown to some, he had started on the two-mile walk to Jerusalem. On the way, he sent two of his disciples to a local village to get a young donkey. The directions were specific: 'Go to the village ahead of you, and as you enter it, you will find a colt tied there, which no one has ever ridden. Untie it and bring it here. If anyone asks you, "Why are you untying it?" tell him, "The Lord needs it"' (Luke 19:30-31).

It happened just as he had told them. Some of the details have been withheld from us. Who was the donkey's owner? Was he, too, a follower of Jesus Christ? Had there been a prior arrangement? Verse 33 indicates there was no prior agreement between Jesus and the animal's owner. Nor did the owner know why the Lord wanted the donkey. The disciples, too, were ignorant of the Lord's intended use of the animal. Here is another example of King Jesus expressing his divine authority. His knowledge, too, was supernatural for he even told the disciples the exact location of the donkey; it was tied in front of a house probably situated near a bend where two roads met. He was no ordinary person.

The fulfilment of Scripture

When the donkey was brought to Jesus, the disciples pulled off their thin jackets and placed them on the donkey in order to make a comfortable seat for their Lord. Then Jesus sat on the animal's back. Remarkably, no one had ever ridden the donkey before and it was unaccustomed both to crowds and noise. However, the one who subdued the storm on the lake, healed the paralysed man, gave sight to the blind and raised the dead was able to ride the untamed animal without any difficulties. But why use a donkey to enter Jerusalem? Was he tired? No, tiredness was not the reason. The answer is threefold.

First of all, he was fulfilling Old Testament prophecy. Over 400 years earlier, God had foretold in Scripture that his Son would enter Jerusalem in this way:

> Rejoice greatly; O Daughter of Zion!
>   Shout, Daughter of Jerusalem!
> See, your King comes to you,
>   righteous and having salvation,
>   gentle and riding on a donkey,
>   on a colt, the foal of a donkey
>
>   (Zech. 9:9).

This prophecy, like others, was fulfilled by the Lord Jesus.

Secondly, the mention of Jesus as 'King' here gives us another clue as to why he used the donkey to enter Jerusalem. Not only was he to be given a royal welcome by the people, but the people should recognize that he was a royal person — God the Son, the King of the universe.

Thirdly, as the donkey was used extensively by the poor and never for purposes of war, our Lord's use of the animal points to his humility and meekness.

A large crowd had gathered to accompany Jesus to Jerusalem. They used their own coats to carpet the road as a token of respect and homage to their leader. Before they reached the outskirts of the city, another crowd of pilgrims joined the procession behind the Lord Jesus. And they were all chanting the praises of Jesus.

The Lord weeps

At this point, something unexpected happened. The Lord began to cry when he saw the city immediately ahead of him. It was a remarkable moment. There was a sharp contrast, too. While the crowds joyfully praised and welcomed him, he himself wept (Luke 19:41-44). The Greek word used here expresses a deep crying and sobbing. His distress was real.

Why? He felt deep concern for the people in the city. They
were blind to his message and mission. Although they were
religious, they did not recognize, or believe on, the Son of God
who was now with them. In fact, they would soon demand his
crucifixion.

But there was more. He foreknew a situation nearly forty
years ahead. To be precise, it would be in A.D. 70. In that year
there would be a great massacre of Jews by the Roman
soldiers. The whole city, including the temple, would also be
destroyed. For these reasons, the Lord wept when he saw the
city and, for those few minutes, paid little attention to the
excited talk and praise of the crowds.

A royal welcome

Now the moment had come to enter the city in triumph. The
people were ecstatic in their praise once they saw Jesus Christ.
They seemed delighted to see him. With palm leaves in their
hands, they waved to welcome Jesus into their royal city.
Almost the whole city stopped to greet and acclaim him.

The scene reminds me of the time when Queen Elizabeth II
visited my home town. With hundreds of other people, my
young children, their grandmother and I stood for almost an
hour at the side of the main road waiting for the queen to pass.
Eventually, a police motorcyclist appeared, followed shortly
by a police car. Only yards behind was an impressive Rolls
Royce car with the queen sitting in the rear, smiling and
waving to the people. All around me, flags were waving and
people cheered. There were shouts, too, of 'Hooray!', 'God
save the queen', and so on. But within a few seconds, the royal
car disappeared from sight and the crowds started to disperse.
The queen had received a rapturous welcome.

The entry of the King

You can imagine, therefore, what it was like when Jesus Christ entered the city of Jerusalem. Obviously there was no Rolls Royce or police car this time. No, there was only a donkey, but a donkey ridden by a very special person, one greater than a queen — Jesus Christ, the Son of God. And there was a rapturous welcome for him from the people. The crowds 'began joyfully to praise God in loud voices for all the miracles they had seen' (Luke 19:37). Their praises of Jesus had a common theme and aim. The same key words recurred in the varying choruses of praise: 'Hosanna', 'Blessed...', 'King', 'Son of David' (cf. Matt. 21:9; Mark 11:9-10; Luke 19:38; John 12:13). It was as a royal person that they welcomed him into Jerusalem. He was King. They also acclaimed him as the Messiah, the anointed one of God chosen to rescue his people. To emphasize the point, the people quoted from Psalm 118:25-26 in order to express their praises of Jesus as King and Messiah:

> Blessed is the king who comes in the name of the Lord!
> Peace in heaven and glory in the highest!

To conclude the chapter, an important fact needs to be underlined, namely, that there is an inseparable link between the Lord's triumphant entry into Jerusalem and his crucifixion. It was no accident that he entered the city.

The significance of the triumphal entry

His visit was deliberate and purposeful. Way back in Luke 9:51 we read that 'Jesus resolutely set out for Jerusalem.' Primarily, he entered Jerusalem, not to receive the praises of people but to give his life a ransom for many. The cross was ahead of him and only in this way could he rescue his people.

His entry into Jerusalem has an additional significance. Just as he had entered the city publicly, so he would die publicly in that same city and on a cross. All would see him die. His unique sacrifice of himself as our sin-bearer would not be done secretly or in a corner.

Certainly the enthusiastic welcome given to Jesus on his entry to the city was the last straw for the religious leaders. They now made detailed plans for his arrest and crucifixion. Over the next chapters these developments and their significance will be traced.

9.
The cup

After the royal welcome to the city of Jerusalem, the Lord
Jesus returned that Sunday evening to Bethany (Mark 11:11).
There he again had food and rested for the night. On the
Monday morning, he walked back to Jerusalem and spent most
of the day in the temple. But the Lord did not like what he saw
and heard.

The scene in the temple

The outer part of the temple had been turned into a market-
place by ruthless businessmen. Admittedly, their business was
related to the temple worship. One group of traders, for
example, sold sheep and oxen to the many worshippers for the
purpose of sacrifice. It was a prosperous business, too. The
prices of these animals were excessively high in order to
exploit the worshippers. Some people would have brought
their own animals from home but the priests were more likely
to accept the animals for sacrifice if they had been bought in
the temple. The reason was obvious. Both priests and businessmen shared the profits.

    Can you imagine the scene? There was the noise and smell

of the animals. Crowds of people also stood around anxious to inspect and buy an animal. It was important that there was no physical defect in the animal they bought for sacrifice. People jostled for a better view of an animal and tried to negotiate the price. The noise was deafening. Nearby, men sold pigeons and turtle-doves to those who could not afford to sacrifice an animal.

In the same area, sitting behind small tables, were men who exchanged foreign currencies. It was a useful provision but here again there was exploitation. A significant number of the worshippers came from other countries in the Roman Empire and the rule was that foreign currencies were not acceptable within the temple area. A further complication was that the Temple Tax had to be paid by each person and money was demanded before people could participate in the various religious ceremonies. However, payment had to be made in Jewish currency.

This was the scene which confronted the Lord Jesus on that Monday. After a period of observation, he intervened dramatically and unexpectedly. Overturning the tables full of money, he drove out the money-changers, as well as the animals and their owners, from the outer sanctuary of the temple. Quoting from Isaiah 56:7 and Jeremiah 7:11, the Lord also shouted out: 'Is it not written: "My house will be called a house of prayer for all nations"? But you have made it "a den of robbers"' (Mark 11:17). A building intended only for fellowship with God, praise and meditation had been turned by these people into 'a den of robbers'. The Lord was insistent and refused to 'allow anyone to carry merchandise through the temple courts' (Mark 11:16).

Almost immediately, however, the crippled and blind people came to him in the temple (Matt. 21:14). With compassion and authority, he welcomed and healed them. Children also came running into the temple shouting his praises: 'Hosanna to the Son of David!' (Matt. 21:15).

The impact of these events

The impact of these incidents was immediate. Already hated by the Jewish religious leaders, the Lord Jesus was now in even greater danger. Active steps were taken by the chief priests and scribes as they 'began looking for a way to kill him' (Mark 11:18). There was a major problem for them: the people admired Jesus Christ and enjoyed listening to his teaching (Luke 19:48; Mark 11:18). How then could they kill Jesus? It was a question they pondered deeply over the next couple of days.

That Monday evening, the Lord Jesus again returned to Bethany for rest and food. The next three days were equally busy and demanding for him.

One day was given over almost completely to discussion with the Pharisees on basic religious, political and moral issues. They wanted to know, for example, his authority for acting as he did in the temple the day before (Matt. 21:23-27). There was a deceitful question, too, about taxes to Caesar. It was part of a scheme by the Pharisees and Herodians to obtain evidence with which they could have him lawfully killed (Matt. 22:15-22), but they were outmanoeuvred by a brilliant answer. The Sadducees then questioned him about the resurrection and again they were left floundering when their ignorance and unbelief were exposed by the Lord (Matt. 22:23-33). Other groups came to ask questions with the intent of trapping him (Matt. 22:35-45).

Most of the time on the Wednesday and Thursday was given over to teaching his own disciples and preparing them for his death, resurrection and ascension. Some of this teaching is recorded in Matthew chapters 24 and 25; John chapters 13-16 and other passages.

The Passover

Thursday was an important day. That evening the Passover meal was due to be observed throughout the country. It was a special occasion. The Passover recalled the historical deliverance of Israel from slavery in Egypt. 'Passover' comes from a verb meaning 'to pass over' and, therefore, to spare; this is what actually happened when God killed the first-born in the Egyptian families but passed over the Israelite houses which had been sprinkled with blood on the outside.

At the command of Jesus, two disciples went to prepare a room for the Passover meal and also purchase the necessary food items, such as bread, a lamb, herbs and wine. The meal had to be observed, in families or in groups varying in size from ten to twenty people, in the early evening. Prior to the meal, the Lord Jesus washed the feet of the disciples, despite protests from Peter (John 13:1-17), and the lesson of humility was impressed upon them. The actual meal went without incident, that is, apart from the treachery of Judas Iscariot. Predicting the betrayal by Judas, the Lord announced, 'One of you is going to betray me' (John 13:21). Although none of the disciples suspected Judas, the Lord Jesus knew all about his plans to betray and assist in his arrest. 'What you are about to do,' warned Jesus Christ near the end of the meal, 'do quickly' (John 13:27). Immediately, Judas left to put his plan into operation.

About this time, Jesus took a loaf of bread in his hand. As he did so, the eyes of all the disciples were focused on him. First of all, he gave thanks for the bread, then he broke it and gave it to the disciples saying, 'This is my body given for you, do this in remembrance of me' (Luke 22:19). He was, of course, using picture-language here. The bread was a picture of his own body which was to be weakened and crucified the next day. In a similar way, the Lord took a cup of wine and explained, 'This cup is the new covenant in my blood, which is poured out for you' (Luke 22:20). The word translated 'poured out' implies a violent death. Matthew, in his account of the incident, adds the words, 'for the remission of sins' (Matt. 26:28, AV). His sacrifice was 'for many' (Mark 14:24) and for sin. In other words, it was a purposeful and sacrificial death.

Gethsemane

The meal probably ended at about 9.00 pm on the Thursday evening. Taking the eleven disciples with him, Jesus walked to the eastern side of the city and across the brook Kidron (John 18:1) to the private garden of Gethsemane. The name 'Gethsemane' means 'olive press' so this secluded garden was probably an olive orchard. Leaving eight of his disciples near the entrance, the Lord Jesus took three into the garden for company and fellowship. He urged the three men to watch and pray while he himself prayed alone a few yards away.

This incident is recorded in each of the four Gospels. In John's Gospel, only one verse is given to it (John 18:1) because John focuses more attention on the Lord's arrest in the garden. Matthew and Mark in their Gospels provide us with the most detailed accounts of what happened in Gethsemane (Matt. 26:36-46; Mark 14:32-42) . Luke's narrative is more concise and concentrates on the manner in which the Lord prayed (Luke 22:39-46). For example, Luke reports that the Lord Jesus, 'prayed more earnestly, and his sweat was like drops of blood falling to the ground' (v. 44). To appreciate this fact we need to remember that Jesus Christ was praying outside in the garden on a cold evening between 10.00 pm and midnight. It was so chilly outside that the soldiers, and even

Peter, warmed themselves in front of a fire in the courtyard (Luke 22:55). To perspire so profusely, therefore, on such a cold evening indicates the intensity with which Jesus prayed. There was extraordinary pressure weighing heavily upon him.

Why was he under such pressure? What was bothering him? How did he feel at this time? We are left in no doubt as to the Lord's feelings. Matthew reports that as Jesus entered the garden, 'He began to be sorrowful and troubled' (Matt. 26:37). Mark quotes Jesus as also saying, 'My soul is overwhelmed with sorrow to the point of death' (Mark 14:34). He was filled with horror and mental anguish as he anticipated suffering and dying the next day in our place on the cross. Weeks earlier he had explained: 'I have a baptism to undergo, and how distressed I am until it is completed!' (Luke 12:50). Here 'baptism' is being used figuratively by the Lord to describe how he would be plunged into deep distress and overwhelmed by agony, as well as desolation, until he was able to shout victoriously from the cross, 'It is finished' (John 19:30). To die for us was no easy option for him; rather, it was costly and distressing.

The cup

But what was bothering the Lord Jesus? Why did he feel such pressure on him? An important clue is provided in the prayer he prayed in Gethsemane. A summary of the prayer, which he prayed three times, is recorded by Luke (Luke 22:42). The prayer is addressed to the 'Father', with whom Jesus was equal and co-eternal and yet who was a distinct person. Here is his request and burden in prayer: 'If you are willing, take this cup from me...' The 'cup' refers to his indescribable agonies on the cross the next day. For example, there was the physical agony of crucifixion, which in itself was dreadful; it was certainly not a pleasant death. What was even worse than the physical pains for the Lord Jesus was the punishment he had to receive from the Father only because he was our substitute.

> He was pierced for our transgressions,
>   he was crushed for our iniquities;
> the punishment that brought us peace was upon him,
>   and by his wounds we are healed...
> and the Lord has laid on him
>   the iniquity of us all
>
> (Isa. 53:5-6).

From eternity the Father, Son and Holy Spirit were together in the unity of the Godhead. Their relationship was a perfect one of love and harmony. At his baptism, as we saw earlier, the Father spoke from heaven concerning Jesus, 'You are my Son, whom I love, with you I am well pleased' (Luke 3:22). Now in Gethsemane, however, ominous clouds appeared in this relationship. No, the Father and Son did not stop loving each other. Nor was Jesus guilty of any sin, or worthy of punishment. The reason for the dark clouds was very different. The Lord Jesus had come at the command of the Father to save sinners. He would do this only by bearing, himself, their punishment fully and finally on the cross. In other words, the cup to which he refers is the cup of God's wrath.

An example from Isaiah 51:17-22 further identifies the 'cup' as being the cup of God's wrath. The chapter is addressed to godly believers in Judah who are urged to trust the Lord. Because of sin, God had poured out the cup of his wrath in judgement upon Judah and this small nation had been compelled to drink it: '... you who have drunk from the hand of the Lord the cup of his wrath' (v. 17). However, in grace the Lord sovereignly removed that cup from them:

This is what your Sovereign Lord says,
   your God, who defends his people:
'See, I have taken out of your hand
   the cup that made you stagger;
from that cup, the goblet of my wrath,
   you will never drink again'

                                           (Isa. 51:22).

Revelation 16:19 throws yet more light on the prayer by similarly identifying the cup with God's wrath. In Revelation 16, 'seven bowls' of divine wrath are poured out on earth; the seventh bowl refers to the final day of judgement and the complete overthrow of sin (vv. 17-21). On this last day, the day of the Lord, the cup of God's wrath will be poured out fully upon unbelievers; it will be terrible and painful: 'God remembered Babylon the Great and gave her the cup filled with the wine of the fury of his wrath' (v. 19).

It is the 'cup' of God's wrath, then, to which the Lord refers in prayer and from which he shrinks. It was not the mere physical pain which made him recoil. Rather it was the awful fact that even he, the Son of God, would be forsaken in his human nature by the Father while he endured the just, divine punishment for our sins. In Gethsemane, therefore, Jesus Christ was crushed to the limit in anticipation of all that lay ahead of him.

We note thankfully that there was more to the prayer. 'Yet,' or 'nevertheless', he adds, 'not my will, but yours be done.' The Greek text expresses it even more strongly: he wants the Father's will to 'be constantly done'. He did not object to, or rebel against, the divine plan; here was a prayer of complete submission and obedience. And it was not mere words either. Within hours, he began to drink the cup of suffering and woe.

The arrest

When he had finished praying, Jesus returned to awaken his sleeping disciples. Almost immediately, a crowd of men led by Judas Iscariot entered the garden. It was a mixed group. Many of the men were armed Roman soldiers from the nearby fortress, while others were temple police armed with cudgels. They were all carrying torches and lanterns. It was then that Judas stepped forward to kiss Jesus several times; this was a pre-arranged signal to the soldiers, indicating the identity of the man who should be arrested.

Knowing what was about to happen, the Lord Jesus walked towards the soldiers saying, 'Who is it you want?' (John 18:4). Their answer was brief and to the point: 'Jesus of Nazareth.' Immediately, the Lord replied, 'I am he.' On hearing this, the captors fell backwards onto the ground and seemed overwhelmed both by the presence and words of Jesus Christ. Once again he asked them the object of their search and repeated, 'I told you I am he... If you are looking for me, then let these men go.'

And so the arrest was made, but only after Peter had tried to resist it. Producing what was probably a dagger, Peter attacked one of the captors, cutting off his right ear. The Lord Jesus was not impressed, nor did he require such help. 'Put your sword away!' he commanded Peter. 'Shall I not drink the cup the Father has given me?' (John 18:11). The agony of Gethsemane was now behind him. Jesus was intent on drinking the cup of wrath given him by the Father. Now the Good Shepherd was about to die for his people, and he would die willingly and obediently. Jesus, therefore, allowed himself to be led away for trial, torture and crucifixion.

10.
A court case

Innocent people are still arrested and accused of crimes they do not commit. Occasionally, a court sentences innocent folk to years of imprisonment or even death. In recent years, there have been several such examples in the United Kingdom alone. A shop manageress, for example, was murdered in South Wales in 1985. It was a most brutal and horrifying crime. The raped woman died from multiple injuries followed by strangulation; her body had even been dowsed in petrol.

Miscarriage of justice

Two brothers were soon charged and found guilty in court of this murder, even though no blood was found on their clothes. Sadly, mistakes were made by the police and there were many irregularities in the case. The brothers spent six years in prison but, with new evidence, a further investigation was ordered by the authorities. All the evidence pointed to the fact that the brothers were innocent; as a consequence, their conviction was quashed and they were released from prison.

There have been other similar cases, such as 'the Birmingham Six', 'the Tottenham Three' and 'the Guildford Four', which have become famous in the United Kingdom. In October 1989 the latter group was freed but only after spending fifteen years in jail. Judith Ward also spent eighteen years in jail for terrorist crimes she did not commit. Campaigners in Great Britain for the reform of the criminal justice system have warned that these high profile cases represent only the tip of the iceberg. Between 1990 and 1992 alone, for example, at least forty people were released from prison because of misleading or inadequate police and scientific evidence, uncorroborated confessions and non-disclosure of material to defence lawyers.

Against this contemporary background, we can appreciate the miscarriage of justice with regard to the trial and punishment of Jesus Christ. He was also punished for crimes he never committed. Here, the powerful religious leaders exploited their legal system in order to ensure that this prisoner received the death sentence. Even when Pilate, the Roman governor, declared Jesus innocent and planned to release him, the leaders pressurized Pilate to reverse his decision and authorize the punishment of crucifixion. The Roman governor lacked the courage needed to ensure that the accused had a fair trial. We shall now look at this court case in more detail.

The hearing before Annas

There were, in fact, two trials awaiting the Lord Jesus: one trial was religious and domestic, whereas the other was a civil, Roman trial. From the garden of Gethsemane where he had been arrested, the Lord was taken in the early hours of the morning to the house of Annas (John 18:13). Here the prisoner was questioned informally.

Annas was seventy years old at the time and an extremely influential person in the country. He had served as high priest and his five sons succeeded him in turn in holding this prestigious office. Caiaphas, the current high priest, was actually his son-in-law. Annas was ambitious, ruthless and worldly; like his colleagues and relatives, he disliked what Jesus did and taught. He first 'questioned Jesus about his disciples and his teaching' (John 18:19). Were there many followers? What was he teaching? How revolutionary were his ideas? Was he undermining the authority of Annas and his colleagues as religious teachers? Could he be the leader of a secret, militant organization? These were the questions which obviously concerned Annas. 'I have spoken openly to the world,' Jesus replied. 'I always taught in synagogues or at the temple, where all the Jews come together. I said nothing in secret. Why question me? Ask those who heard me. Surely they know what I said' (John 18:20-21). The Lord's answer was gracious and factual but firm, and the former high priest needed to be reminded of the facts.

Although this was not legal, Annas now decided with others to convene, during the night, an emergency meeting of the Jewish parliament. He felt the situation was urgent, so messengers were sent to call the members together. Annas also sent Jesus, 'still bound, to Caiaphas the high priest' (John 18:24). Over fifty members of parliament came to the house of Caiaphas and sat in a semi-circle with Caiaphas as chairman sitting on a slightly elevated chair in the centre. Immediately in front of Caiaphas stood the prisoner, Jesus Christ, flanked on either side by police officers. Behind Jesus stood a mixed group of men prepared to tell lies in evidence against the prisoner.

False evidence

The religious trial was quickly under way. After questioning Jesus about his teaching, the high priest called for people to give evidence against the Lord. Many were prepared to fabricate evidence against Jesus in order to have him sentenced to death; however, no two persons agreed on their evidence. Finally, however, two men came forward and claimed, 'This fellow said, "I am able to destroy the temple of God and rebuild it in three days"' (Matt. 26:59-61). They were referring to an occasion nearly three years earlier when the Lord had said something similar (John 2:19). However, they misquoted and twisted the Lord's words, which were, 'Destroy this temple, and in three days I will raise it up.' He was in fact referring to his own death and resurrection, not to the rebuilding of the temple in Jerusalem. Once again his enemies had fabricated the evidence.

The Son of Man

Caiaphas, the high priest, was now angry. Getting up from his seat, he challenged Jesus with two questions: 'Are you not going to answer? What is this testimony that these men are bringing against you?' (Matt. 26:62). To the amazement of the questioner, the Lord Jesus 'remained silent'. Caiaphas could restrain himself no longer: 'I charge you under oath by the living God: Tell us if you are the Christ, the Son of God' (v. 63).

The Lord's reply was immediate and affirmative: 'Yes, it is as you say.' In this reply, he used a Hebrew idiom which Matthew records precisely while Mark, in his account of the incident, translates the idiom as, 'I am,' in order to avoid any possible misunderstanding (Mark 14:62). What is striking, however, is that the Lord proceeded to give a more detailed answer than was required: 'But I say to all of you: In the future you will see the Son of Man sitting at the right hand of the Mighty One and coming on the clouds of heaven' (Matt. 26:64).

On hearing those words, 'The high priest tore his clothes.' This was not a spontaneous outburst of anger but a traditional way for religious leaders to indicate that they had listened to blasphemy. 'He has spoken blasphemy!' he shouted out. 'Why do we need any more witnesses?' (Matt. 26:65). Caiaphas had understood the significance of the answers from the Lord. Terms like 'Christ', 'Son of God' and 'Son of Man' were pregnant with meaning. 'Christ' means 'the anointed one', the Messiah and long-awaited deliverer. Caiaphas links the title 'Christ' with that of 'Son of God' in his question to Jesus; the latter title, 'Son of Man', expresses the Lord's unique relationship with the Father. He is the 'only ("alone of its kind") Son' (see John 1:14,18; 3:16,18). The rich Old Testament background, especially of Daniel 7:13, highlights the significance of the 'Son of Man' title; it refers to the heavenly origin, glory and authority of the Lord Jesus. He was no ordinary person.

The verdict

'Look,' exclaimed Caiaphas to his colleagues, 'now you have heard the blasphemy. What do you think?' (Matt. 26:65-66). The verdict of the parliamentary members was unanimous: 'He is worthy of death.'

What happened next was unlawful and cruel. Not only was Jesus refused a fair trial, but he was also assaulted as a prisoner and ridiculed. There was no protection for him. Those who had pronounced him guilty and worthy of death began to spit in his face and hit him with their fists. Others were content merely to slap him and then, blindfolding him, to ask, 'Prophesy to us, Christ. Who hit you?' Eventually, the guards intervened but only to take him outside to beat him themselves.

The religious court in the house of Caiaphas the high priest had now finished its business. A unanimous verdict had been reached: the accused must die. At this stage, there was nothing the court could do but to transfer the prisoner to the Roman authorities. Only minor religious offences could be handled by the Jews in their own court. Rome alone had the right to decide whether a prisoner should be sentenced to death or not. Jesus, therefore, was taken to the Roman governor immediately.

Pilate

Pilate was the Roman governor of this southern part of Palestine and as such was directly responsible to the emperor in Rome. Although a married man with considerable admin-istrative experience, he lacked the courage and wisdom needed at times to make unpopular decisions. His relationship with the Jewish leaders was also strained. To make matters worse, the Jews resented the Roman occupation of their country. Whether they liked it or not, however, the Jewish court needed Pilate's authorization to kill Jesus Christ.

The civil trial was held either in the governor's palace or in rooms which the governor used in a fortress situated near to the temple. Their religion would not allow the religious leaders to enter a pagan building, so they handed Jesus over to the Roman soldiers near the entrance in order not to defile themselves. Even though it was still very early in the morning, Pilate came out to them and asked, 'What charges are you bringing against this man?' (John 18:29). Their reply was pointed: 'If he were not a criminal, we would not have handed him over to you.' When Pilate advised them to judge the prisoner by Jewish law, they objected that they had no right to execute anyone. They wanted no less than the death sentence for the Lord Jesus. At this point, the Bible declares that 'This happened so that the words Jesus had spoken indicating the kind of death he was going to die would be fulfilled' (John 18:32). The divine plan was now going to be accomplished as the Lord Jesus died on the cross on behalf of sinners.

But the court case had not ended yet and Pilate had still not sanctioned the death sentence. In fact, the trial and intrigue continued for a few more hours and this will be described in the next chapter.

11.
The case continued

Law experts in the United Kingdom have expressed concern over the way people suspected of having committed a crime are sometimes treated by the police. Some suspects, for example, have either been forced into making false confessions or exposed to prolonged 'mental beating'. In fairness, however, it must be pointed out that the police are under tremendous pressure on occasions to secure a conviction. Perhaps it is the abuse or murder of a child, the rape of a young woman, a brutal attack on a defenceless person, or the bombing and shooting campaign of political terrorists which make an outraged public demand instant police success in finding the guilty persons.

For example, a twenty-year-old prostitute was savagely stabbed more than fifty times and had her throat slit on St Valentine's Day, 1988. People felt angry when they heard about the murder and wanted the guilty person or persons to be apprehended quickly. Well, the police arrested five men, three of whom were jailed for life. Late in 1992, the Appeal Court in London released these three men and the appeal judges expressed their horror on hearing of the 'sledgehammer' interrogation techniques used by the police with regard to one of them. The defence lawyer claimed that the man had been 'seduced' into confessing and then only after 103 denials that he did it and following thirteen hours of intense grilling. 'It was nothing short of bullying,' he added. 'It is not an attempt to search for the truth. Their single objective was to ensure, so far as they could, and by using means short of actual physical violence, to achieve a confession. They ridiculed and demeaned him. They used emotive language of the highest sort. This man was reduced to a state of distress and tears.' While mistakes made by the police must be acknowledged, the question still remains, were police officers in this murder enquiry pressurized to secure a successful conviction?

Pilate under pressure

That there was pressure on Pilate to sentence Jesus Christ to death is beyond dispute. There was what experts now distinguish as 'institutional pressure', with the religious leaders uniting to compel the Roman governor to comply with their wishes. These leaders also helped to create the 'public pressure' which finally forced Pilate's hand in the matter. They also exerted 'political pressure', too. This is seen in the main charge brought against Jesus, namely, that he had set himself up as a rival king. The complaint to Pilate was that he 'claims to be Christ, a king' (Luke 23:2). Pilate could not, therefore, ignore the charge because of its serious political implications.

There were two other charges brought by the Jews which the Roman governor ignored. One, that Jesus perverted the nation, was vague and lacked credibility. Another charge, that Jesus forbade people to pay tax to the Roman government, was a downright lie. Only a couple of days earlier, a group of Pharisees and Herodians had questioned him whether or not it was right to pay taxes to Cæsar (Matt. 22:17). His reply was firm and clear: 'Give to Cæsar what is Cæsar's, and to God what is God's' (Matt. 22:21). Significantly, the Jewish leaders did not mention to Pilate the charge of blasphemy on which they had condemned Jesus earlier in their ecclesiastical trial. They were now applying 'political pressure' in order to force Pilate to sentence their prisoner to death.

The cross-examination

After hearing the charges brought against Jesus, Pilate took him inside the building for cross-examination.

'Are you the king of the Jews?' was the first question from the Roman official.

'Yes, it is as you say,' replied the Lord Jesus (Matt. 27:11).

John's account of the cross-examination reveals that Jesus immediately asked Pilate whether his question about kingship was asked for personal reasons, or merely for the official purpose of the trial. It was a searching question and a necessary one. Was Pilate himself a seeker and eager to find out the truth about Jesus Christ? Here was a glorious opportunity for the governor to find the only way to God and salvation. Sadly, Pilate indignantly replied, 'Do you think I am a Jew?' He had no personal interest either in Jesus or in the concerns of the Jews. 'It was your people and your chief priests who handed you over to me' (John 18:35). Pilate was just doing his job and trying to reach a judicial decision with regard to the guilt of Jesus.

This led him to ask the next question: 'What is it you have done?' Was there any truth in what the Jewish leaders said against Jesus? He needed to be sure on this point although he shrewdly suspected that it was 'out of envy' that the Jews had handed over this prisoner to him (Mark 15:10).

Christ the King

Now it was time for the Lord Jesus to explain in more detail the nature of his kingship. Yes, he was a king but, he insists, 'My kingdom is not of this world' (John 18:36). He was no rival to Cæsar. If he had been, then his servants would have fought to resist his arrest a few hours earlier. 'But now my kingdom,' he explains, 'is from another place,' that is, it does not find its origin or authority in people, countries or governments of this world.

There was now an immediate interruption from Pilate who had noticed the Lord's reference to a 'kingdom'. The Lord's use of that word 'kingdom' was deliberate; the Greek word *'basileia'* has the basic meaning of 'kingship', 'rule', and does not refer to a region or empire, so there could be no possibility of Jesus rivalling Cæsar for his throne. However, the Roman governor was wary and interjected: 'You are a king, then!' (John 18:37). He did not fully grasp what Jesus was saying.

'You are right in saying I am a king,' Jesus replied. Pilate needed, however, to understand the sense in which Jesus was king and for this reason he was immediately given more information. 'For this reason I was born,' said Jesus, 'and for this I came into the world, to testify to the truth.' As God and as the appointed rescuer of sinners, Jesus was born King and came from heaven in order to unveil the facts concerning God and his salvation. No one was better qualified to do this than Jesus Christ.

Pilate, therefore, was in a privileged position at that moment and he was challenged even further to take advantage of this privilege: 'Everyone on the side of truth listens to me.' Here was an invitation to Pilate and to anyone else to listen to the important message which Jesus had brought. If Pilate was searching for the truth then he would listen and believe on

Jesus. His response was disappointing; rather cynically he retorted, 'What is truth?' Was Pilate too busy or even afraid to hear the truth? Or did he not want to listen any more to Jesus?

Whatever the explanation may have been, the Roman official was at least convinced of Jesus' innocence. He went out immediately and informed the Jewish leader, 'I find no basis for a charge against him' (John 18:38). He had made the right decision and reversed the verdict of the Jewish religious court.

'He did not open his mouth'

Nevertheless, Jesus was not released because of the pressure exerted by the Jews on Pilate. Luke reports that they brought new charges against Jesus: 'He stirs up the people all over Judea by his teaching,' they insisted. 'He started in Galilee and has come all the way here' (Luke 23:5).

By this time, the Roman official was perplexed as to what he should do next. Turning to Jesus, he asked, 'Don't you hear the testimony they are bringing against you?' 'Aren't you going to answer? See how many things they are accusing you of' (Matt. 27:13; Mark 15:4). To the astonishment of Pilate, 'Jesus made no reply, not even to a single charge' (Matt. 27:14).

This was not the first nor the last time for Jesus to be silent in front of his accusers. Only a couple of hours earlier he had remained silent when charged in front of Caiaphas the high priest (Mark 14:60-61). Later, when sent to King Herod (Luke 23:9) and when he appeared a second time before Pilate (John 19:9), he again chose not to answer the accusations made against him.

We are not told the reasons for this silence. Certainly, however, the Lord Jesus was fulfilling Old Testament prophecy, which had predicted centuries earlier that 'He did not open his mouth' (Isa. 53:7; 42:1-4). Perhaps, too, Pilate did not need an answer for he was already convinced of the prisoner's innocence.

Herod

As he thought about his next step, Pilate recalled that the Jews talked of Jesus starting his teaching in Galilee. This gave him an idea for a possible way forward. Herod was the ruler of the Galilee area and he was actually in Jerusalem for the Passover celebrations. Could Herod advise about this case, or even give his verdict? It seemed a sensible thing to send Jesus chained to Herod Antipas for his opinion.

But what kind of man was Herod? He was an able administrator and a keen architect, but he had few moral scruples. Leaving his own wife, he committed adultery by taking his brother's wife, Herodias, and this action had earned for him earlier a severe rebuke from a famous preacher, John the Baptist. Herodias was also a strong character and kept Herod under her own control.

Seeing Jesus, however, Herod 'was greatly pleased' (Luke 23:8). He knew about Jesus and had wanted to see him for a long time. One of his hopes was to see Jesus perform a miracle. In a relaxed and friendly manner, Herod plied him with many questions and carried on talking.

Once again Jesus did not speak a word by way of reply or explanation, even though the Jewish leaders stood nearby, 'vehemently accusing him'. His silence was embarrassing but effective. Herod could not be respected as a man because of his adultery. Nor did the ruler have any genuine interest in religion or God. For he had previously heard John the Baptist preach and call him to repentance but the message had fallen on deaf ears. Now the Lord Jesus stood in front of him as a prisoner. However, there was no trial or consideration of the charges against Jesus, as Pilate had intended. There was, therefore, no need for Jesus to answer.

Before returning the prisoner to the Roman governor, Herod dressed Jesus in an elegant robe and joined the soldiers in ridiculing and mocking him. It was a gesture of contempt and a reference to the charge that he claimed to be a king. Laughing in unison, the soldiers and religious leaders took Jesus back to Pilate's headquarters.

Pilate seeks a compromise

Pilate's plan had not succeeded but he was still determined to release the innocent prisoner. Calling the Jewish leaders to him he immediately announced: 'You brought me this man as one who was inciting the people to rebellion. I have examined him in your presence and have found no basis for your charges against him. Neither has Herod, for he sent him back to us; as you can see, he has done nothing to deserve death' (Luke 23:14-15). His mind was made up. If Jesus was innocent then justice demanded he should be released immediately. However, a compromise of some kind seemed inevitable in the circumstances. The compromise was that Jesus should be punished before his release. And it seemed a reasonable compromise to Pilate, but the Jews did not agree. They still wanted Jesus to be crucified.

There was, however, another possibility for Pilate. Each year the Roman governor released a prisoner, and the large crowd outside demanded a prisoner to be released. The governor acted quickly and gave a choice to the people between Jesus Christ and a notorious murderer and rebel named Barabbas. Under the influence of their leaders, they shouted in favour of Barabbas. A shaken Pilate replied, 'What shall I do, then, with Jesus?' (Matt. 27:22-23). The answer was clear and

united: 'Crucify him!' Another two questions from Pilate
went unheeded: 'Why? What crime has he committed?' Even
louder this time, the people demanded that Jesus should be
crucified.

Seeing that 'he was getting nowhere', and that a riot was
starting, Pilate washed his hands in a basin of water for all to
see, declaring, 'I am innocent of this man's blood. It is your
responsibility' (Matt. 27:24). He had eased his own conscience
and registered his unwillingness that Jesus should die, but
unperturbed the crowd replied, 'Let his blood be on us and on
our children!'

The Son of God

At this point, Jesus was handed over to the soldiers for
flogging. Did Pilate still want to release his prisoner? Was this
his reason for telling the religious officials, 'You take him and
crucify him. As for me, I find no basis for a charge against
him'? (John 19:6). But it was not the end of the matter. Now
the Jewish leaders mentioned for the first time the original
charge for condemning Jesus, namely, his claim to be the Son
of God.

Hearing this, Pilate returned inside to question the prisoner
again: 'Where do you come from?' Once again there was no
answer from Jesus Christ. 'Do you refuse to speak to me?'
Pilate added. 'Don't you realize I have power either to free you
or to crucify you?'

This time an answer was required, so Jesus explained to the
Roman ruler, 'You would have no power over me if it were not
given to you from above' (John 19:11). Even Pilate, the Jewish
leaders and everyone else were under the authority of the
sovereign God. Jesus would die on the cross because of God's
plan, not at the whim of Pilate or as a helpless victim of

circumstances. There was also understanding and sympathy in the Lord's response to Pilate when he explained, 'The one who handed me over to you is guilty of a greater sin.' After all, the Roman ruler had not initiated or encouraged the case against Jesus, nor did he want him crucified. In fact, he tried several times to release this remarkable prisoner but in vain.

A final warning

A final warning from the enemies of Jesus to Pilate ended all attempts to obtain the prisoner's release. 'If you let this man go,' the Jews shouted to Pilate, 'you are no friend of Caesar. Anyone who claims to be a king opposes Caesar' (John 19:12).

Pilate was frightened. He did not welcome the idea of a complaint against him being sent to Rome; it could have spelt the end of his career. Here was political pressure forcing Pilate to yield to their request for the crucifixion of Jesus. He acted quickly. Taking the prisoner outside, he announced, 'Here is your king.'

'Take him away! Crucify him,' was the response of the people.

'Shall I crucify your king?' Pilate asked.

The chief priests answered, 'We have no king but Caesar' (John 19:15). They were playing politics for their own evil ends.

Suffering, torture and crucifixion now awaited Jesus, the Son of God, as Pilate handed him over to the soldiers.

12.
Suffering, torture and crucifixion

Early in 1945, several concentration camps in Germany were liberated by Allied forces. For millions of Jews and Poles, however, the rescue came too late. British soldiers found 40,000 prisoners in a camp near Belsen, many of whom were dying from starvation, typhoid and tuberculosis. There were also hundreds of naked, rotting corpses heaped up in different locations of the camp. One such heap was of unclothed women prisoners who had died weeks earlier; nearby, children were playing.

After the capture of Buchenwald concentration camp, American personnel struggled for months to save the lives of 20,000 prisoners. Many of these prisoners had been used as medical 'guinea pigs' and subjected to surgery without anaesthetic. On the camp was a portable scaffold used by the Germans to hang prisoners publicly.

By June 1945, German civilians were taken on forced visits to these Nazi camps to see for themselves the evidence of torture and mass extermination committed by the Nazis. Coachloads of civilians were taken to see the gas chambers and ovens in which hundreds of thousands of victims were cremated, often while still alive. Visitors saw piles of human ashes, unburned bones, torture equipment used by guards and toys taken from children before they were herded into the gas chambers or ovens. Machines were strategically located in order to reduce the noise of human screams.

Similar torture and atrocities were committed by the Japanese in their prisoner-of-war camps. British, Dutch and Australian soldiers died from disease, starvation or slave-labour in these camps. Those who survived were seriously emaciated and reported that they had been given frequent beatings, deprived of vital medicines and forced to do heavy manual work in tropical heat and on a tiny allocation of food per day.

The torture of Jesus

Although it took a different form, nevertheless, the Lord Jesus Christ also suffered considerable cruelty and torture. On the Thursday evening, he had been handcuffed in the garden of Gethsemane during his arrest by the temple police and Roman soldiers. Once arrested, Jesus was taken to the house of Annas, an old but influential man who had once been high priest. While he was being questioned there, 'One of the officials near by struck him in the face' (John 18:22). The slap was delivered by one of the temple policemen who acted on his own initiative and no doubt with the motive of pleasing his superiors. During the night immediately after the religious court had pronounced a sentence of death, those guarding Jesus turned to poke fun at him and hit him hard repeatedly with the palms of their hands. That was not all. To express their contempt, they spat on him, then blindfolded the prisoner before teasingly demanding, 'Prophesy! Who hit you?' (Luke 22:64). 'And they said many other insulting things to him.'

The flogging

Now came the authorized flogging. It was Pilate who ordered Jesus to be flogged when he realized that the religious leaders and the public preferred to have a murderer and rebel like Barabbas released rather than Jesus. While the decision to beat Jesus was a concession to the people, it was also part of Pilate's plan to release Jesus later. A cruel torture weapon was used by the soldiers to flog prisoners. The weapon was a short piece of wood which had several pieces of rope and leather fixed to it. Attached to the pieces of rope and leather were pointed lumps of lead and sharp stones. It was a nasty weapon. The soldiers made Jesus bend over before beating his bare back many times with the weapon. The flogging lasted for several minutes until the prisoner was wounded and, usually, the veins and inner organs exposed. It was not a pretty sight and already the Lord Jesus was in great pain.

The mock coronation

Following the scourging, Jesus was handed over by Pilate to the soldiers for crucifixion. The Lord Jesus was led away by the soldiers to their own barracks and they immediately called on all their colleagues to join in the fun. Mark reports that they 'called together the whole company of soldiers,' that is, a group of 600 men. Although Roman soldiers, they were probably natives of the province of Syria and conversant with the Aramaic language spoken by the Jews and with their customs. On occasions like a crucifixion, Roman soldiers were allowed some freedom in provoking and teasing their condemned prisoners. Certainly they lost no time in playing a game of 'let's pretend' in the courtyard.

The game was really a mock coronation, indicating that they had discussed among themselves the charge that Jesus claimed to be a king. One of the first things the soldiers did was to disrobe him, then put an old purple-coloured coat worn by soldiers over Jesus as a gesture suggesting royalty. The action of throwing the coat around an already bleeding and wounded body must have been extremely painful for Jesus Christ. Next, they collected some long, sharp spikes from a nearby shrub and pressed them down onto his head in the shape of a crown suitable for a king of the Jews. By this time, blood was running down his face and body. It was a cruel game. For a sceptre, they used a stick which was given to the Lord Jesus to hold. Now that he was attired in the semblance of a king, the soldiers began to march past their prisoner, saluting, laughing and calling out, 'Hail, King of the Jews' (Mark 15:16-20). Probably they went on bended knees in turn to give him mock homage. They also slapped him, spat in his face and, taking the stick out of the Lord's hand, 'struck him on the head again and again' (Matt. 27:26-31).

'Led like a lamb to the slaughter'

Rather hurriedly in the end, the soldiers removed the purple coat and put his own clothes back on before leading him out to be crucified. We need to notice how often in the Gospel narratives we are told that Jesus allowed himself to be 'led', 'led away', 'sent' and 'brought' by the Jews and the Roman officials during these hours. Centuries earlier it had been prophesied that Jesus would be 'led like a lamb to the slaughter' (Isa. 53:7).

Without doubt, Jesus was in complete control of the situation and would die willingly for his people. 'I lay down my life... No one takes it from me,' he had explained earlier, 'but I lay it down of my own accord' (John 10:17-18).

Carrying the cross

The order had now been given by Pilate: Jesus must be crucified. Although we cannot be sure of the precise location for crucifixion, we know it was always outside the city. The soldiers, therefore, had to walk their condemned prisoner at least a mile. It was also the prisoner's duty to carry the cross. It was exhausting, carrying such heavy beams of wood through the narrow, crowded streets of the city. But there was help available, as one of the soldiers showed mercy. Perhaps seeing the exhaustion of Jesus and aware of his gaping, bleeding wounds, he felt sorry and ordered an onlooker to carry the cross instead of Jesus. The man must have been shocked to receive such a command. Simon was his name and he was from North Africa, Libya to be precise, and he was just visiting the city for the religious festival. Matthew tells us that it was while Jesus, with his escorts, enemies and friends, was walking out of the city that Simon was forced to help.

Crucifixion

Within a short time, they reached the place of crucifixion called Golgotha, which is a Greek version of the Aramaic name *golgoltha* meaning a skull. It was the Vulgate, the first Latin translation of the Bible, which translated the Greek word for skull *(kranion)* as Calvaria, from which we have the English Calvary.

More important than the name, however, is what actually happened there. Almost immediately the soldiers tried to give Jesus a bitter drink of myrrh and wine to lull his senses and ease the excruciating pain of crucifixion. The drink was refused because the Lord Jesus wanted to feel the full extent of the pain ahead of him and to remain fully conscious in order both to speak from the cross and offer his life willingly as our substitute.

The time was now about 9.00 a.m. on the Friday morning. It had been a long, exhausting night but the soldiers were now ready to crucify Jesus. Those who died on a Roman cross were always naked, so the soldiers removed his clothes and probably threw a dice in order to decide how the various items of clothing were to be shared among them. The cross consisted of two rough wooden beams. Probably Jesus had to lie down first of all on top of the cross and then the soldiers drove large nails through his hands and feet before placing the cross, with its victim, upright in the ground.

The torture of crucifixion was slow and could last for as long as three days but for Jesus the physical pain and torture lasted for only five or six hours. While hanging on the cross, the Lord Jesus suffered severe inflammation, the swelling of wounds in the hands and feet, excruciating pain from torn tendons, intense thirst and considerable ridicule.

Ridicule

The ridicule came from various groups of people. For example, there were those walking past who shook their heads in scorn and 'hurled insults at him,' saying, 'So! You who are going to destroy the temple and build it in three days, come down from the cross and save yourself!' (Mark 15:29-30). Another group who mocked Jesus consisted of the chief priests and scribes: 'He saved others,' they shouted out, 'but he can't save himself! Let this Christ, this King of Israel, come down now from the cross, that we may see and believe' (Mark 15:31-32). Luke tells us that these people 'sneered' at Jesus in hatred (Luke 23:35).

The policy of the Romans was to use crucifixion as the ultimate punishment for slaves and criminals who had committed dreadful offences. On this occasion they had taken the opportunity to crucify two other people at the same time as Jesus. These two men were criminals and deserved their punishment. At first, even these two criminals, as they hung helplessly on their crosses, hurled insults at Jesus Christ until one of them had a change of heart and repented.

From all directions, people mocked and poked fun at the Lord Jesus, yet he never retaliated, nor did he attempt to defend himself or tell them off as they deserved. Peter tells us, 'When they hurled their insults at him, he did not retaliate; when he suffered, he made no threats. Instead, he entrusted himself to him who judges justly' (1 Peter 2:23), and in this respect he is an example to believers how they should themselves respond when insulted and unjustly treated (1 Peter 2:21). Edward Denny has expressed this well in his hymn:

What grace, O Lord, and beauty shone
Around thy steps below!
What patient love was seen in all
Thy life and death of woe!

For ever on thy burdened heart
A weight of sorrow hung,
Yet no ungentle, murmuring word
Escaped thy silent tongue.

Thy foes might hate, despise, revile,
Thy friends unfaithful prove:
Unwearied in forgiveness still,
Thy heart could only love.

O give us hearts to love like thee,
Like thee, O Lord, to grieve
Far more for others' sins than all
The wrongs that we receive.

Spiritual suffering

Over the six hours that Jesus hung on the cross, his sufferings increased under the intense heat of the sun. More of these details will be given in the next chapter, but we need to underline a point of major importance before closing this chapter. Worse than all the torture, ridicule and pain of the trial and crucifixion were the spiritual sufferings Jesus endured for us. These sufferings are impossible for us to measure, or even adequately describe. On the cross, Jesus Christ died as our substitute and bore the punishment due to our sins. But this involved for him degrees of punishment, forsakenness and darkness which only he could have borne as the Son of God. While drinking the cup of God's wrath on the cross, he exclaimed, 'My God, my God, why have you forsaken me?' (Matt. 27:46). The significance of those words will be explained shortly but for now let us note that the physical sufferings of Jesus, although dreadful and extensive, were yet only a small part of what he endured in order to rescue sinners.

13.
Parting words

To enable us to appreciate even more the spiritual as well as the physical sufferings of Jesus Christ, we shall concentrate in this chapter on his parting words. While hanging on the cross, Jesus spoke seven times and each time his words were of enormous significance.

There are two details which need to be remembered concerning these sayings of Jesus Christ. First of all, in the first three sayings from the cross the Lord concentrated on the concerns and needs of other people around him, namely, his persecutors, the repenting thief and his own mother, Mary. By contrast, in the last four sayings he was preoccupied with his own concerns as he died in the place of his people. There is no contradiction, however, between these two groups of sayings, for in both the Lord Jesus was lovingly and unselfishly concerned for people. Even when he refers to his own thirst or sense of being forsaken in the second group of sayings, this was in the context of his loving, and dying for, the church. He was not hanging on the cross as a punishment for his own sins or crimes, for he was without sin. Even Pilate admitted his innocence in the civil trial. His only reason, therefore, for being on the cross was to rescue sinners from hell and reconcile them to God.

A second detail concerning the seven sayings of Jesus on the cross also deserves a mention at this point. Between the two groups of sayings, there was a break of three hours. During that time, Jesus Christ was silent and, even though it was only early afternoon, darkness covered the land. Was this God's direct action for the purpose of hiding the awful sufferings of his Son? Although the Lord Jesus did not answer the insults of his enemies, God the Father did by miraculously sending a dense darkness which lasted from noon until mid-afternoon. It was towards the end of this period of darkness that the Lord Jesus spoke his last words from the cross.

1. Father, forgive them, for they do not know what they are doing' (Luke 23:34)

These first words of Jesus were spoken soon after he had been nailed to the cross. For several reasons, they are remarkable. One reason is that even in the time of greatest distress and suffering, Jesus continued to trust completely in the Father and to pray to him. He did not pray to himself, angels or saints, but to God the 'Father' with whom he was co-equal and co-eternal.

Another reason why these words of Jesus are remarkable is the request they contain: 'Father, forgive them.' Can you imagine it? Jesus had nothing but love in his heart towards the many people who in different ways had mocked and hurt him. He desired that they should be forgiven, not punished, by his Father.

Over forty years ago a Korean Christian forgave a young Communist official for killing his son. It was a genuine act of forgiveness, for when the official was eventually captured and sentenced to death by American soldiers, he pleaded for his release and took him as an adopted son into his own family. Similarly, in the early 1990s in Northern Ireland a man whose daughter was killed by IRA terrorists announced publicly that he felt no hatred at all towards the terrorists. 'I forgive them,' he declared, 'even though they killed my daughter.' Are these two cases unusual? Yes, they are, but these two men were Christians and only the Lord's grace enabled them to express love, not bitterness, towards the murderers of their children.

You would need, however, to multiply their love millions of times in order to approximate to the love of Jesus; his love is like a vast ocean compared with the small river of love expressed by believers. William Rees, a Welsh hymn-writer who died in 1823, captured this thought admirably:

Here is love, vast as the ocean,
Loving-kindness as the flood,
When the Prince of life, our ransom,
Shed for us his precious blood.

Another hymnist, Samuel Trevor Francis, writes of:

... the deep, deep love of Jesus!
Vast, unmeasured, boundless, free,
Rolling as a mighty ocean...

The one who had instructed his disciples to love their enemies, pray for their persecutors (Matt. 5:44) and even forgive until seventy times seven (Matt. 18:22) here provided a glorious example of love and kindness. His prayer was answered in a remarkable way, for many of the people who insulted and crucified him were themselves converted later. About 3,000 of them trusted in Christ through Peter's sermon at Pentecost (Acts 2:41) and also each day individuals were converted. Weeks later thousands more became believers and then 'A large number of priests became obedient to the faith' (Acts 6:7).

In the next saying, we shall see that Jesus' love reaches individuals who are not only enemies but also criminals.

2. 'Today you will be with me in paradise' (Luke 23:43)

Joining in the insults being hurled at Jesus were two criminals who were crucified on either side of him. 'Aren't you the Christ? Save yourself and us!' (Luke 23:39) taunted one of these criminals. By this time there was a change in the attitude of his colleague. He had probably been impressed by the love of Jesus expressed in the prayer, 'Father, forgive them...' Now he recognized that Jesus was innocent and a special person, indeed a Lord with a kingdom. The inscription, 'This is the king of the Jews' (Luke 23:38), above the head of Jesus appeared to this repenting criminal to be a major understatement. On top of all this, he was conscious of his own guilt and sin.

The other criminal must have been startled to receive a rebuke from his colleague: 'Don't you fear God, since you are under the same sentence? We are punished justly, for we are getting what our deeds deserve. But this man has done nothing wrong' (Luke 23:40-41).

Almost immediately the speaker called out, but this time to the Lord himself, 'Jesus, remember me when you come into your kingdom.' While the other criminal was concerned only that Jesus should rescue him from crucifixion, this man wanted the Lord Jesus to save him eternally. He was going to die and face a holy God and wanted to obtain a place in heaven. Was it possible? Could a criminal be saved? 'I tell you the truth,' Jesus replied, 'today you will be with me in paradise' (Luke 23:43). What glorious words! A condemned criminal who had robbed and killed was now forgiven and saved. How was it possible? After all, he had no time to go to church, be baptized, go to Holy Communion, or improve his life. It was possible only because the man's sin and punishment were being taken and paid for by a substitute, Jesus Christ. There is no other way. Our response to Christ and his sacrifice is really a matter of life and death for us. And that is what this repenting criminal found out.

3. 'Dear woman, here is your son... Here is your mother'
(John 19:26-27)

It was his concern for Mary, his mother, which prompted Jesus to speak on this third occasion from the cross. Even while dying, he was thinking of his widowed mother. A small group of women, including Mary, stood near the cross together with John the disciple. It must have been agony for them to see Jesus hanging on a cross. And there was nothing they could do to change the situation or to alleviate his pain. Unable to give him a drink or wipe the blood off his face or bathe his wounds, Mary could only stand helplessly waiting for the inevitable end.

Unexpectedly, Jesus then addressed her with the words, 'Dear woman, here is your son.' Four times in the immediate context of verses 25-27, John uses the word 'mother' with regard to Mary, but Jesus did not use the word at all. Instead, he used here a term of respect and affection which can be translated as 'dear woman'. His choice of word was deliberate. Did he want to make it easier for Mary to cope emotionally with the situation and so avoid using the emotive term 'mother'? Perhaps he was teaching her an important lesson, too. Although privileged to be his mother, Mary was still a sinner who needed grace and forgiveness through the cross. Was she now being prepared to rely on her spiritual rather than physical relationship to her Saviour?

Jesus is also setting us an example here in at least two ways. Firstly, we must, like Jesus her son, be restrained when we talk about Mary. Titles like 'Mother of God' and 'Queen of heaven' are extravagant titles and are not authorized either by Jesus himself or the Bible. Secondly, Jesus sets us an example in honouring our parents (see also Exod. 20:12; Eph. 6:1-3). By telling his disciple John, 'Here is your mother,' Jesus made practical arrangements for her care and protection. 'From that time on,' we are told, 'this disciple took her into his home' (John 19:27). And she was greatly helped in this way.

4. 'My God, my God, why have you forsaken me?' (Matt. 27:46)

These words help us to appreciate further the spiritual sufferings of Jesus Christ on the cross. Remember that from noon until three o'clock in the afternoon darkness had descended over all the land; this occurred at a time, of course, when the sun should have been giving maximum light and warmth. One immediate effect of the darkness was to restrain the insults of the crowd and it also gave Jesus more privacy in which to suffer and die. The darkness may also have been a picture of God's judgement upon sin; both physically and spiritually, it was a horribly dark afternoon.

It was near the end of this three-hour period of darkness that 'Jesus cried out in a loud voice, ... "My God, my God, why have you forsaken me?"' He was quoting the opening words of Psalm 22 in order to describe his sense of desolation, abandonment and suffering. This was an awful moment. And it is the word 'forsaken' which provides the clue to what happened. Jesus had already been forsaken by the crowds and even by his own disciples. This was something which he had predicted beforehand to his disciples: 'You will be scattered, each to his own home. You will leave me all alone' (John 16:32). Yet he added these significant words: 'Yet I am not alone, for my Father is with me.' His comfort throughout the years was his Father's presence and fellowship. The climax of his being forsaken, therefore, was the cross, where Jesus felt forsaken even by the Father. 'God forsaken by God?' asked Martin Luther, 'Who can understand that?'

Although we cannot fathom the depths of this experience for the Lord Jesus, it is helpful to notice that it was as our representative, substitute and mediator he spoke these words. God the Father was dealing with him, not as his eternal Son, but as our sin-bearer who, on the cross, was being punished in our place. 'The wages of sin is death' (Rom. 6:23); this means not only physical death but also separation from God. Bearing such awful punishment for us, the Lord Jesus was deprived of the sense of God's presence and consolation; it felt as if he had been abandoned and left without support. Here was indescribable, unimaginable suffering.

5. *'I am thirsty'* (John 19:28)

This is the only expression of physical need and pain spoken by Jesus on the cross. Already he had hung on the cross for nearly six hours. His last drink had been about twenty hours earlier but a lot had happened to him in the meantime. He had walked to the garden of Gethsemane, perspired in prayer there, then had been marched by soldiers to the houses of Annas, Caiaphas and Pilate. All through the night his court case had continued and he had even been taken to see King Herod. After Pilate sentenced him to be crucified, he was flogged, then forced to walk over a mile to Golgotha and carry his own cross for part of the way. He was exhausted and wounded. Immediately before crucifixion, Jesus refused a drugged drink because he wanted to remain conscious throughout his sufferings. For three hours he then hung on the cross under the intense heat of the sun and when darkness descended for the following three hours Jesus felt desolate as he was punished for sin. Now his work was almost finished and his death imminent. Exhausted, he declared, 'I am thirsty.' In this way, he fulfilled Old Testament prophecy (see Ps. 22:15; 69:21) concerning himself and showed also the reality of his human nature; he was the God-man. Fully identified with us in his human nature, he knows our needs, limitations and suffering better than anyone.

To quench the Lord's thirst, a soldier kindly soaked a sponge in some bitter wine before attaching the sponge to a stick long enough to reach Jesus' mouth. The sponge was then probably squeezed repeatedly against his mouth to enable him to drink.

6. *'It is finished'* (John 19:30)

As soon as Jesus finished drinking the wine, he shouted out this word of victory for all to hear. What had he finished? He had fulfilled over 300 distinct prophecies in the Old Testament relating to his rescue mission and sufferings. There were four prophecies concerning his death which still waited to be fulfilled: namely, his committing of himself to the Father (Ps. 31:5; Luke 23:46); the piercing of his side with a spear (Zech. 12:10; John 19:34-37); that his bones should not be broken (Ps. 34:20; John 19:36); and his burial in a rich man's grave (Isa. 53:9; John 19:3-42). His mission, too, in coming into the world was now accomplished, his physical sufferings were at an end and his atoning sacrifice for sin completed. He had met all the requirements of God's holy law for us; all our sins had been laid on him and he bought our salvation perfectly and finally. Although it had been costly yet he could now say, 'It is finished.'

7. *'Father, into your hands I commit my spirit'* (Luke 23:46)

Here are the final, parting words of Jesus before he died. There is an obvious contrast between his words here and his prayer in Gethsemane or on the cross when he expressed his sense of being forsaken by God. Here all is calm, the darkness has gone, the cup of wrath has been drunk and his work is finished.

This calmness of Jesus can be described in four ways. It is the calmness of *achievement*. From eternity, he had carried a heavy responsibility by being appointed to care and die for the elect to secure their salvation. Now the work was finished. There is also the calmness of *anticipation*. Because of his obedience to the death of the cross, he would soon enter upon his reward as mediator by his resurrection, ascension and session at the right hand of the Father. Earlier he had announced, 'I came from the Father ... now I am leaving the world and going back to the Father' (John 16:28). Therefore, 'For the joy set before him [he] endured the cross, scorning its shame' (Heb. 12:2). Calmness of *affection* is also expressed in these words. Jesus was equal, and intimate, with the Father and Holy Spirit but for the first time ever there was a cloud in this relationship as he bore our sins on the cross. Now that fellowship had been restored. Finally, we see the calmness of *assurance* as he committed himself into the hands of his Father. Within seconds, 'He breathed his last' (Luke 23:46) and died — in his human nature.

14.
Dead and buried

Jesus Christ died. This basic, historical fact is emphasized repeatedly throughout the New Testament. 'Christ died for the ungodly... Christ died for us... We were reconciled to him through the death of his Son' (Rom. 5:6,8,10). 'Christ Jesus, who died...' (Rom. 8:34). 'Christ died for our sins' (1 Cor. 15:3). 'He ... became obedient to death — even death on a cross!' (Phil. 2:8). 'We believe that Jesus died...' (1 Thess. 4:14). 'He suffered death' (Heb. 2:9). 'He has died as a ransom' (Heb. 9:15). 'For Christ died for sins once for all' (1 Peter 3:18).

The Lord Jesus Christ also spoke unambiguously concerning his own death: 'I lay down my life for the sheep' (John 10:15). He also predicted his death on several occasions. For example, only weeks before his crucifixion he gave more details about his sufferings and death to the twelve disciples: 'Everything that is written by the prophets about the Son of Man will be fulfilled... They will mock him, insult him, spit on him, flog him and kill him' (Luke 18:31-32; see also further references in Matt. 16:21; 17:22,23; 26:1-2; Mark 8:31; 9:31; 10:32-34; Luke 9:22). The biblical evidence is overwhelming; Jesus Christ died, and he died on a cross.

Confusion among Muslims

Although the Koran mentions the death of Jesus Christ, Muslims are divided in their opinion as to whether Jesus died or not. One of their problems concerns the interpretation of the word *'inni mutawaffeeka'* in verse 55 of Surat al Imran which is translated as 'gathering thee'. Some deny that the word means 'death' and prefer to interpret it as 'sleep', 'fulfilment' or 'taking possession of'. It is suggested by some that Jesus will first vanquish the Antichrist and only then will he die and 'Muslims will bless him' (Abu Jaafar al Tabari). Those Muslims who accept that the word in question means a real physical death still have different explanations of it.

To add further to the confusion for Muslims, there are three texts in the Koran which acknowledge the death of Jesus Christ and two of these texts declare that he was killed (see Surat al Mariam 33, Surat al Imran 55, 183, Surat al Baqara 87). The first reference here clearly teaches that Jesus Christ was incarnate, died and was raised from the dead.

It is to the Bible, the Word of God, that we must turn for reliable information concerning the facts and significance of Jesus' death. The Bible's teaching is crystal-clear: Jesus died on a cross.

Evidence for the death of Christ

There is ample proof for the death of Jesus Christ. Normally, the Roman authorities allowed the bodies of those crucified to hang on the cross for hours and even days. Their corpses were exposed to the weather, sometimes torn and eaten by wild birds or burnt. For the Jews, this was intolerable and unlawful. The Old Testament law commanded them: 'If a man guilty of a capital offence is put to death and his body is hung on a tree, you must not leave his body on the tree overnight. Be sure to bury him that same day, because anyone who is hung on a tree is under God's curse' (Deut. 21:22-23). Clearly, there was no choice for the Jewish leaders but to honour this law.

There was another pressure on them as well. The following day was a Sabbath and so there would be a double defilement if the body of Jesus was allowed to remain on the cross until the Sabbath. Moreover, it was a special Sabbath for it was the Sabbath of the Passover feast. In addition, a special sheaf offering was made on the second day of the festival which was the Sabbath.

It was probably the chief priests who went along to Pilate requesting that the legs of Jesus and those of the two criminals should be broken in order to hurry the process of death. If that was achieved then the bodies could be taken down and the whole sordid affair finished before the Sabbath started. Pilate agreed to the request.

The soldiers normally used a large hammer or a heavy piece of iron to break the legs of those crucified. It was a cruel measure but effective. The two criminals had their legs broken first of all but when the soldiers reached Jesus they found he was already dead. In order to make absolutely certain that he was dead, one of them plunged his spear into the side of Jesus, producing a 'sudden flow of blood and water' (John 19:34-37). We cannot be precise as to which side or part of the side was pierced. One theory that is popularly held is that the spear went through Jesus' heart, so that the blood from the heart joined the fluid from the pericardial sac, which explains the 'flow of blood and water'. Some medical experts have a different explanation: 'It has been shown that where a chest has been severely injured but without penetration, haemor-rhagic fluid, up to two litres of it, gathers between the pleura lining of the rib cage and the lining of the lung. This separates, the clearer serum at the top, the deep red layer at the bottom. If the chest cavity were then pierced at the bottom, both layers would flow out.'[1] Whatever the medical explanation may be, John draws attention to the certainty and reality of Jesus' death; in his human nature, he died.

There is yet more proof. Probably referring to himself, John emphasizes the reliability of this evidence: 'The man who saw it has given testimony, and his testimony is true. He knows that he tells the truth, and he testifies so that you also may believe' (John 19:35).

When the Roman centurion who stood in front of Jesus saw how he died, he exclaimed, 'Surely this man was the Son of God!' (Mark 15:39). Also contributing to this confession were some miraculous happenings which occurred immediately after Jesus died: an earthquake, the breaking of rocks, the resurrection of many dead believers from the graves and the tearing of the thick temple curtain from top to bottom. For the centurion and others assisting him in the supervision of the crucifixion these unusual happenings created fear and even greater respect for Jesus (Matt. 27:51-54). All nature seemed to register the fact of Jesus' death.

Secular historians provide further proof that Jesus died. Tacitus was a Roman historian writing approximately in A.D. 115 concerning the persecution of Christians in A.D. 64 by the Emperor Nero. During the detailed history, Tacitus refers to 'Christus ... who was executed at the hands of the procurator Pontius Pilate in the reign of Tiberius.' Even earlier, about A.D. 93, a famous Jewish historian, Josephus, who was not a Christian, wrote in his *Antiquities of the Jews*, 'About this time there arose Jesus, a wise man ... a doer of wonderful deeds and a teacher... He was the Christ; and when Pilate, on the indictment of the principal men among us, had condemned him to the cross, those who loved him at the first did not cease to do so, for he appeared to them again alive on the third day.'

There is no doubt about it; Jesus died and died on a Roman cross.

To suggest that Jesus did not die, but merely fainted or collapsed into unconsciousness on the cross, does not fit the facts. It would have been impossible for so many people to be deceived about Jesus' death, some of whom were soldiers experienced in the art of crucifixion; in addition, there were the Jewish enemies who were vigilant in ensuring beyond all possible doubt that Jesus was dead. Although Jesus was already dead before he was pierced by the soldier's spear, nevertheless the piercing confirmed that he was dead.

His burial

At this stage in the narrative, our attention is drawn to Joseph. His home was in Arimathea, a small town about twenty miles north-west of Jerusalem. Joseph was an important man, largely because he was a member of the Jewish parliament, and he was wealthy. He therefore had prestige and influence in the country as well as respect. To understand why Joseph buried the body of Jesus, we need to be aware of three significant facts.

The first is that Mark describes him as a devout person who was looking for God's kingdom to be established (Mark 15:43). In other words, he loved God and longed to see more people trust and obey the Lord. His faith was real.

A second point to notice is that he was a secret disciple of Jesus Christ. The reason for the secrecy was that Joseph feared what his colleagues might do to him if they found out that one of their number was a follower of Jesus. The thought of it had probably terrified him.

Another interesting fact is that Joseph did not support the Sanhedrin's decision to condemn and crucify Jesus (Luke

23:51). In this he was consistent but then he did not say or do anything at the trial to prevent Jesus from being crucified.

Now, however, he was courageous. On his own initiative he went to the Roman governor with a request that he be allowed to take and bury the body of Jesus. There is no doubt that if the relatives of Jesus had made this request they would have been refused. For Joseph it was different; he was one of the Jewish leaders. But did he provide Pilate with the opportunity he needed to annoy and snub the enemies of Jesus by looking favourably on Joseph's request? Surprised to hear that Jesus was already dead, Pilate summoned the centurion to him who then confirmed the fact that Jesus was dead. At once, Joseph was permitted to take Jesus' body.

Accompanying Joseph was Nicodemus, a colleague in the Sanhedrin who had himself talked with Jesus Christ secretly early in his ministry. Nicodemus also emerges as another secret disciple. Their rôles here were complementary. Joseph was the organizer and spokesman who dealt with the official and legal aspects of obtaining the body of Jesus. While he also provided the linen cloth in which the body of Jesus was wrapped, it was Nicodemus who had brought an expensive mixture of spices which was placed inside the linen cloth. When all the preparations were completed, the body was taken to a garden conveniently near Golgotha and placed carefully in a new tomb which was likely to have been a small cave. A large stone was then moved across in order to seal the entrance to the tomb. Jesus was now buried as well as dead.

The significance of the burial

As we might expect, the burial of Jesus is full of significance. For one thing, it was the fulfilment of a prophecy given over 700 years earlier: 'He was assigned a grave with the wicked, and with the rich in his death' (Isa. 53:9). The Lord Jesus himself had also prophesied that he would be buried. To the unbelieving Pharisees, Jesus had said, 'For as Jonah was three days and three nights in the belly of a huge fish, so the Son of Man will be three days and three nights in the heart of the earth' (Matt. 12:40). Over the weekend as Jesus lay buried in the tomb, this prophecy was literally fulfilled.

In his burial, Jesus Christ was also still bearing the punishment of our sin in the sense that physical death and the grave are part of God's curse upon sin. On our behalf, he surrendered himself to death and the grave. Here was the final and lowest stage in his humiliation, yet what a great contrast there was here! Jesus Christ is the one 'who alone is immortal' (1 Tim. 6:16); that is, he has endless existence as God and he is the one who gives and sustains both physical and spiritual life. As God the Son, he is the very opposite of death, yet through the marvel of his incarnation he was able and willing to die in his human nature for the purpose of saving us. Ann Griffiths, a famous Welsh-language hymn-writer of the eighteenth century describes the contrast in this stark way:

> They put the Author of life to death
> And buried the Great Resurrection.

Thanks be to God, that is not the end of the story. On the third day he rose triumphantly from the tomb and this will be the theme of our next chapter.

---

1. Quoted by D. A. Carson, *The Gospel According to John,* IVP, 1991, p.623.

15.
Alive again!

'Coco the dog is back from the dead.' This was the title of an article in my daily, regional newspaper some time ago. It was not only my love of dogs that made me read the article; I was also intrigued by the title. What had really happened to Coco? Well, Coco was a two-year-old cross Springer Spaniel who had been lost for seven months, probably stolen. His owner missed him greatly and grieved after him. She thought the dog was dead. Eventually, her son called at a local dogs' home to choose a replacement dog for his mother but there, furiously wagging his tail and with a quizzical look on his face, was Coco. 'I just couldn't believe my eyes,' he said, 'we had given up the dog for dead — but there he was, still clowning around.' His owner was overjoyed at seeing Coco again: 'I was crying with delight because we really thought he was dead,' she admitted.

It makes an interesting and moving story, but of course, Coco never died at all and he did not return from the dead although, metaphorically, it seemed like that to the family. And despite the impressive evidence already given establishing the death and burial of Jesus Christ, there are still some critics who deny that Jesus actually died and rose from the dead. They suggest, for example, that the whole thing was a hoax on the part of the friends or the enemies of Jesus. However, the suggestion is absurd. If the enemies of Jesus had stolen his body as a hoax, why did they not produce it when they tried to stop the apostles preaching the resurrection of Jesus Christ? Or would the friends of Jesus have been willing to go to prison and even die just for a hoax? Others suggest that Jesus did not die at all. What happened, they say, is that he fainted and went into unconsciousness only to revive again after several hours in the cold tomb. This theory was dealt with in the last chapter so there is no need to repeat the answer except to emphasize that the soldiers, as well as the disciples and the Jewish leaders, were satisfied beyond all possible doubt that Jesus was really dead. Were they all wrong? After all, it was in the interests of the Jews and Pilate to be sure that Jesus was dead. Unlike Coco the dog, the Lord Jesus really did die and came back from the dead.

Jesus is alive!

Pastor Richard Wurmbrand of Romania relates the story of a Russian soldier who discovered a small piece of paper in a field. The soldier was intrigued because the piece of paper was obviously part of a book and the words interested him. In fact, he was so impressed with the words that he made an effort to memorize many of the verses on the bit of paper. Not knowing that the paper belonged to the New Testament — in fact it contained parts of Matthew's Gospel chapters 5 and 6, which we call the Sermon on the Mount — the soldier asked many of his friends if they recognized the words and knew which book they belonged to, but no one could help him.

Eventually, the soldier met Richard Wurmbrand, who was able to explain that his piece of paper came from the Bible and the words were first spoken by Jesus Christ. Over several hours, Wurmbrand told him about the teaching of Jesus, his miracles and his great love for people. The soldier was impressed. Wurmbrand then mentioned the sufferings and death of Jesus on the cross and the Russian was distressed. He had not heard anything about Jesus Christ before. For him, Jesus was such a wonderful person that it was difficult to imagine that people would want to kill him. Tears rolled down his cheeks as Wurmbrand went on to explain that Jesus died as a substitute for sinners and that this rescue work necessitated his dying. Seeing the sadness of the soldier, Wurmbrand reassured him: 'That was not the end; Jesus rose again from the dead!' Excitedly, the soldier jumped to his feet to express his joy on hearing this news. He was right: it is glorious news; Jesus is alive from the dead.

Evidence for the resurrection

There is firm evidence to show that the resurrection of Jesus Christ really took place. It is not a myth or a fairy story. Just think of all the people who saw and heard Jesus after his resurrection. Some of them, like Thomas, refused to believe until they had convincing proof. 'Unless I see the nail marks in his hands,' said Thomas, 'and put my finger where the nails were, and put my hand into his side, I will not believe it' (John 20:25). Thomas refused to believe without firm evidence. It was another eight days before he met Jesus, who invited him to 'Put your finger here; see my hands. Reach out your hand and put it into my side. Stop doubting and believe' (John 20:27). Only then was Thomas convinced and he replied, 'My Lord and my God!'

The apostle Paul also marshals convincing evidence for the resurrection of Jesus in 1 Corinthians 15:5-8. Peter, James and all the apostles saw Jesus alive after his resurrection. On one occasion, about 500 people met and talked with Jesus after his resurrection. Most of them were still alive when Paul wrote his letter and he suggests that doubters could go and question these people about what they saw.

Only six weeks after the resurrection of Jesus, the apostle Peter proclaimed with joy Christ's resurrection: 'God has raised this Jesus to life,' and he went on to emphasize, 'We are all witnesses of the fact' (Acts 2:32). Those early believers could vouchsafe for the historicity of the claim that Jesus was alive again. The Christian faith is built on facts; the facts are historically verified and, therefore, reliable.

In 1930, Frank Morison wrote a book with the title, *Who Moved the Stone?* His original intention in writing the book was to ridicule and disprove the resurrection of Jesus Christ, or at least cast doubt on its historicity. Morison examined all the evidence in minute detail but was eventually compelled to acknowledge that Jesus had indeed been raised from the dead. He was overwhelmed by the impressive evidence in favour of the resurrection of Jesus. For example, both the friends and enemies of Jesus alike admitted that the tomb was empty. If the enemies had actually removed the body of Jesus then they would have disclosed its whereabouts, especially when the apostles began to preach powerfully the fact of his resurrection. Also significant for Morison was the fact that even the disciples were not expecting Jesus to be raised to life; in fact, they found it hard to believe until they actually saw and heard Jesus in person. Morison, the cynic, was convinced that Jesus rose from the dead.

A physical resurrection

The Lord Jesus, then, in his human nature was raised to life on the third day and his body glorified. A number of people in churches, or in cults such as the Jehovah Witnesses, deny the physical resurrection of Jesus.

The latter, for example, assume that the body of Jesus was destroyed even though the Bible does not say so. To support their unbiblical view, they quote the words of 1 Corinthians 15:50 that 'Flesh and blood cannot inherit the kingdom of God.' But these words do not prove their point at all. The apostle is talking in the context about the resurrection of the dead bodies of Christians when the Lord Jesus returns in glory to the world. These bodies must also be changed, as well as raised, in order to prepare them for the new life in heaven. That is exactly what happened to Jesus Christ in his resurrection. The body of Jesus was changed into a glorified body, and the Lord Jesus when he returns personally will also 'transform our lowly bodies so that they will be like his glorious body' (Phil. 3:21).

Others object that they have never met a person who has been raised from the dead. That is obviously true. Nevertheless, it is also true that we have never seen a person like Jesus Christ. He is unique and it was impossible for death to keep the Son of God in its grip — not even his body. Not only, then, was Jesus alive again, but his body was also raised and transformed.

The significance of the resurrection

His resurrection proved beyond all doubt the truth of all that the Lord Jesus taught in his three-year ministry. His claim to be 'the resurrection and the life' (John 11:25) was not an empty one; his own powerful resurrection and triumph over death vindicated it. His words, 'Destroy this temple' (that is, his body), 'and I will raise it again in three days' (John 2:19), were fulfilled just as he said. Frequently he spoke of going to his

Father (e.g. John 14:12; 16:17,28) and he went, as he said, via the cross, resurrection and ascension. To the disciples at Cæsarea Philippi he revealed that 'He must be killed and on the third day be raised to life' (Luke 9:22). Now this had all been fulfilled; his claims and teaching were all reliable and true.

In addition, he 'was declared with power to be the Son of God by his resurrection from the dead' (Rom. 1:4). Besides being a great victory over Satan and hell, the resurrection of Jesus was God's way of showing that he had accepted his sacrifice for sin. Here is the ultimate proof that Jesus' sacrifice for us was accepted by the Father and that our salvation had been purchased once and for all through his substitutionary death. The resurrection of Jesus is the seal of God upon his death on the cross. His work was not only finished; it also met with the approval of heaven.

The Bible goes further still. Jesus' resurrection lays the basis for, and guarantees, our justification before a holy God: 'He was delivered over to death for our sins and was raised to life for our justification' (Rom. 4:25). His death and resurrection are inseparable. For it is through the living Jesus Christ, and in our intimate union with him, that we are put into a right relationship with God, but only on the basis of his death. Charles Spurgeon suggested in a sermon that if the devil accuses us of all, or even some of our sins, then the Christian should answer, 'Jesus died for my sin and removed it far away from me.' If the devil returns with the same accusations, Spurgeon tells the Christian to respond with the words: 'Jesus *lives,* and his life is the assurance that we are no longer guilty before God: for if our Saviour had not paid our debt, he would still be under the power of death.'

Finally, the resurrection of Jesus is significant because it is a pledge that death has lost its sting for believers. The Bible declares that 'The sting of death is sin' (1 Cor. 15:56). Apart from sin, there would be no death at all (Rom. 5:12). It is sin which gives to death all its terror and awfulness. The reason is that 'The power of sin is the law' (1 Cor. 15:56). Sin is the breaking of God's law, and it is this very law which pronounces us guilty and condemns us to death. 'But thanks be to God! He gives us the victory through our Lord Jesus Christ' (1 Cor. 15:57). He gave perfect obedience to all the demands of the law and conquered death by dying and rising again. 'Because I live,' he declares, 'you also will live,' eternally and gloriously (John 14:19). He, who is himself 'the resurrection and the life', assures us that 'He who believes in me will live, even though he dies; and whoever lives and believes in me will never die' (John 11:25-26). Just as Jesus rose physically from the grave, so all believers will similarly one day be raised and have a renewed body (Phil. 3:21; 1 John 3:2; 1 Cor. 15:51-57).

A glorious resurrection awaits those who belong to Jesus Christ. When and how we die or where we are buried and who officiates at our funeral or what we bequeath to families are unimportant matters compared with our relationship to Jesus Christ. To die without him will be foolish and disastrous; to die trusting him will mean heaven and a glorious physical resurrection as well.

The exaltation of Christ

The resurrection of Jesus must also be seen as the first stage in his exaltation, in which as the living, ruling Head of the church and Lord of the universe, he enables God's chosen people to become Christians and eventually enter glory. Six weeks after his resurrection, the Lord Jesus was talking with the disciples when he was suddenly lifted up from them into heaven (Acts 1:9-11). It was necessary for him to ascend to the Father. As our mediator, he was rewarded and entered into his glory in heaven (Luke 24:26); there, he is our forerunner (John 14:2) and he sends the Holy Spirit to his church (John 16:7). When he ascended, the Lord Jesus was given a position of great honour at the right hand of God the Father and there as mediator he rules over both the church and the entire universe (Heb. 1:3; 10:12; 1 Peter 3:22). It is from this position of absolute power that the Saviour builds and protects his church, prays for believers (Rom. 8:34) and sends the Holy Spirit (Acts 2:33; John 16:7-15).

The climax, however, is yet to take place. One day, no man or angel knows when, the Lord Jesus will return personally to the world. His coming will be visible, not secret or invisible, as Jehovah Witnesses teach. No, 'He is coming with the clouds, and every eye will see him' (Rev. 1:7; cf Matt. 24:30). He will also come in glory, accompanied by angels. His coming has a definite purpose in view, as well. The world will then be judged, the bodies of the dead raised, believers glorified, and the devil and his hosts, together with unbelievers, cast into hell before the Lord makes a new earth and a new heaven from which all traces of evil will be removed. Then, as Jesus Christ publicly owns his people and leads them into heaven, the glorious purposes of God will be consummated.

Make no mistake about it, Jesus Christ is alive. Although we are concentrating in this book on the unique, saving *death* of Jesus, we must never lose sight of his words: 'I am the Living One; I was dead, and behold I am alive for ever and ever! And I hold the keys of death and Hades' (Rev. 1:18).

In the next section of the book, it will be necessary for us to retrace our steps somewhat. Why do we need to be rescued by Jesus Christ? What, if anything, is wrong with us? Are we really sinners? Is there danger ahead of us? These are some of the questions which need to be answered before we go on to explain in greater detail in the fourth section what Jesus actually did on the cross to rescue sinners.

Section III
The cross: man's need

16.
Disaster

Walking around a large bookshop a couple of years ago, I noticed one book which especially caught my attention. It was not the bold blue-and-black cover which attracted me, but the title, *The World's Worst Disasters of the Twentieth Century.* Curious to find out more, I picked up the book and turned immediately to the contents page. There I saw that twenty-eight major disasters between 1902 and 1983 were described in varying detail in the 192-paged paperback. You guessed right! I bought a copy and later read the sad contents.

Which disasters were included in the book? There was the San Francisco earthquake of 1906, when three tremors were felt, separated from each other by only a few seconds, but the third was the worst one. Immediately, 28,000 buildings were destroyed and an area of four miles completely devastated. As many as 450 people were killed. Another disaster mentioned was the story of the *Titanic,* which sank in the Atlantic in April 1912 after hitting an iceberg. Out of the 2,206 people aboard, 1,403 were lost, mostly crew and male passengers. Or there was the London smog of 1952 which killed over 4,000 people. The smog was thick with fumes from industrial waste and lay over the city for nearly three weeks.

Then there was the mass poisoning in Iraq during the years 1971 and 1972. In order to cope with a major famine disaster, the Iraqi government bought wheat germ and barley seeds from Mexico and the United States. However, Iraq insisted that all the grain should be treated chemically with a substance called methylmercury dicyandiamide in order to counteract plant disease. Several other countries had already banned the substance because of evidence that it was lethal to humans and animals. Despite this evidence, Iraqi authorities insisted on using it and many things went wrong with the project itself. As a direct result of this chemically treated grain, experts maintained that as many as 6,000 people in Iraq died and 100,000 were injured although official statistics put the total poisoned at 6,530 and recorded only 459 hospital deaths.

The last disaster detailed in the book was the series of Southern Australian bush fires in February 1983. With temperatures at a record February level of 110 degrees Fahrenheit, there was a high level of risk and in places arson was suspected. For two full days the bush fires spread rapidly, with the help of a strong fifty-miles-per-hour wind, making 8,500 people homeless and devastating 150,000 acres of farm and forest land. More than 200,000 sheep and cattle perished and seventy people also died.

I could not help thinking that the title of the book was misleading and exaggerated. For example, some of the worst disasters I thought of as occurring this century were not mentioned. Was there a greater disaster this century than World War II, with the killing of millions of troops and civilians? What about the inhuman treatment of Jews by the Nazis? I also expected the Hiroshima atom-bomb disaster to be included. Nor did the book record disasters later than 1983. Will the Ethiopian and Somalian famines, Chernobyl, the Armenia earthquake, the sufferings of the Kurds in the Middle East, or the massacre of 70,000 people in Romania prior to the arrest and execution of President Ceausescu at the end of 1989 be included in a later book?

The worst disaster ever

What if we were asked to name 'The World's Worst Disaster Ever'? There would probably be considerable disagreement among historians, politicians and others in identifying it. I wonder what the most popular answer would be? The Bible's answer to the question is clear and emphatic: the world's worst disaster ever was the fall of Adam and Eve. Let me explain this statement in more detail.

God's reliable book, the Bible, takes us back over the centuries to a location in the Middle East and to a time before human civilization developed. Here is the beginning of human history and the time of the first two humans, Adam and Eve. They were the parents of the entire human race; we have all descended from this first man and woman.

Man and woman as God created them

Adam and Eve did not emerge as the result of a chance explosion of gases and a long process of evolution; nor did they descend from the apes or any other creature. Adam, the first man, was created directly by God himself. God made man, too, in a remarkable way. 'The Lord God,' the Bible announces, 'formed ... man from the dust of the ground' (Gen. 2:7; cf 1:26-27; 5:1-2; Matt. 19:4; 1 Tim. 2:13-14). In this unusual way, man was made a physical being, but man has more than a body. The Bible declares that God also made man 'in his own image, in the image of God he created him' (Gen. 1:27). This means that man reflects and resembles God in the

sense that he has a moral, rational and spiritual nature. Unlike
the animals, man is able to reason and knows instinctively the
difference between right and wrong. Unique also to humans is
a spiritual dimension whereby they are able to know and enjoy
God. For these reasons, man is unique and stands as the
pinnacle of God's creation. Eve's later creation by God is
described in Genesis 2:21-25. Both Adam and Eve were
created righteous by God; that is, they had no sin in their lives
and obeyed the Lord perfectly all the time.

Can you imagine such a situation? There was no violence,
selfishness, pride or cruelty in their behaviour. They did not
lie, steal, or lose their temper. Husband and wife got on well
together without speaking harsh words or quarrelling. There
was perfect harmony in their relationship and both individuals
cared unselfishly each for the other. This is how God made our
first parents and they lived in a perfect, harmonious world
without earthquakes, floods and other natural disasters.

Sadly, it was not long before disaster struck. The story of
this disaster is recorded in Genesis chapter 3 while the significance of the event is brought out in Romans 5:12-21.

The entrance of sin into the world

What happened to Adam and Eve? To put it briefly, they both
sinned by disobeying God — Eve first and then Adam. In this
way, 'Sin entered the world through one man' (Rom. 5:12).
Those seven words tell us a lot about the world's greatest disaster ever. 'Sin' is a small but ugly word; it refers to the breaking of God's holy law either in deed, word or thought. Like all
humans, Adam and Eve were under an obligation to obey God
constantly. One of God's commands to them was that they
should not eat the fruit of a certain tree, otherwise they would
be punished by death (Gen. 2:16-17). Nevertheless, tempted
by the devil, they both disobeyed God and sinned.

Notice next that this sin 'entered' the world; it was not there before, nor was it part of human life. And here is a crucial point. A happy, perfect world, created by God, was suddenly spoilt and ruined. Human nature, which had been created clean and good by God, now became dirty and polluted through the disobedience of Adam and Eve. As we shall see in the following chapters, the result was disastrous, not only for Adam and Eve, but also for the history of all mankind. Adam and Eve involved us all in the world's worst disaster ever. All our troubles and problems, whether personal or family, national or international, stem from this one disaster. The only effective remedy for these disastrous problems is the Lord Jesus Christ and his death for us on the cross.

How does it affect us?

You may well have a question in your mind at this point, namely, why must we suffer for Adam's sin? Is it fair? Surely we cannot be blamed and made to suffer for something which Adam and Eve did thousands of years ago! What, then, do we have to do with the world's greatest disaster? The question is reasonable and requires an answer.

The Bible informs us that God chose to deal with the entire human race as one entity in Adam. That was God's wise decision. As Creator of the universe and as God, he had the right to deal with the human race as he pleased. We certainly have no authority to question his decision or criticize him. While Adam was an individual person yet God treated him also as representative of the human race. Whether we like it or not, this is the case; Adam was made the head of the human race and our representative. This means that when Adam obeyed we were represented in his obedience but when he sinned we were all regarded by God as having sinned in Adam. 'And in this way,' the Bible teaches, 'death came to all men, because all sinned' (Rom. 5:12); 'The result of one trespass was condemnation for all men' (Rom. 5:18).

The unity of the human race

I want to illustrate the unity of the human race in Adam in two ways. There were remarkable and emotional scenes in Berlin near the end of 1989. The harsh barriers between east and west Berlin had just been removed and the Berlin wall built by the Communists in 1961 was no longer the insuperable barrier it had been, dividing the people for nearly thirty years. As thousands of East Germans flocked into the west to a tumultuous welcome, the people began to shout spontaneously, 'We are one, we are one, we are one people.' We know what they meant for they shared a common language, culture and history. Before the partition of Germany after World War II, they had also shared one country. However, in a far deeper sense, the peoples of the world are all one. Created by God in his image with Adam as its federal head, mankind is one and God has dealt with us in Adam as one.

A second illustration makes a similar point. Mikhail Gorbachov achieved the highest political position in the former Soviet Union and was largely responsible for encouraging *perestroika* among his people.[1] Outside his country, Gorbachov became known as a politician of world significance who genuinely wanted peaceful coexistence with other nations, especially the West. Gorbachov regarded the world as united because of the ecological problems threatening the health and survival of mankind and this fact in itself contributed substantially to the felt need for peaceful international relations. The unity of mankind was, therefore, an important concept for the former Soviet leader. In the context of East-West relations and the continued quest for disarmament, he illustrated the unity of mankind. He described all humans and their nations as being tied together by a rope, that is, they all belong together and are one despite political, cultural and economic differences. If, said Gorbachov, a person or nation falls, then it is possible that the entire human race would also fall and perish, for they are all inextricably tied together, whether they like it or not, in the one rope of humanity. The point he makes is a valid one. Certainly, in God's purpose, we were all tied together to Adam as a human race when he became our representative and leader. That was God's wise decision, not ours, as God chose to deal with mankind as one entity represented by Adam. When Adam sinned, therefore, he dragged us all into sin with its tragic consequences.

The pollution and danger resulting from Adam's sin will be detailed in the next chapters but we should notice here that the principle of a representative also works to our advantage because the Lord Jesus Christ became our representative and sin-bearer. As our representative, he obeyed the law which we have all broken and also took our punishment upon himself and died to save us eternally. It is the cross and resurrection of Jesus Christ which alone repairs the damage caused by the world's greatest disaster ever.

1. Gerd Ruge, *Gorbachov,* Chatto & Windus, 1991.

17.
Pollution

The news was bad and it dominated the TV news programmes that evening. People were concerned. On the following morning, newspapers carried front-page headlines like 'Pollution Disaster'. It was compulsive reading. What was it all about? Early in January 1993 the giant oil tanker, *Braer,* ran aground in gale-force winds at the remote Quendale Bay, five miles west of Sumburgh in the Shetlands, north of Scotland. All the thirty-four-man crew were plucked to safety by a rescue helicopter. What caused concern was that the supertanker had loaded about 85,000 tonnes of light crude oil in Norway but the oil was now leaking from the vessel's forward tanks and those sited near the engine room. As oil poured into the sea, attempts to board the ship and treat the oil slick were hampered by severe weather conditions and hurricane-force winds. Within days, the tanker broke up into four parts. It was an ecological disaster although the severe weather helped to break up the oil slicks. Plans were made to airlift seabirds polluted by oil hundreds of miles to a specialist cleaning centre on the Scottish mainland, but even the most thorough rescue and cleaning operation failed to save the majority of those rescued. Farmers also reported that the fleece on sheep four miles from the wreck turned brown due to airborne pollution while some local people suffered skin irritation and chest complaints.

Rivers as well as seas can be polluted, and for reasons other than oil disasters. For example, domestic sewage, farm slurry and toxic chemicals are only a few of the many sources of river pollution.

A worldwide problem

The problem of pollution is also worldwide and is so serious that the prosperous industrial democracies have promised a global crusade against it. In Germany and other parts of Europe there is anxiety about the possible effects of air pollution, the ozone layer break-up and acid deposition on forests. The German government estimates that fifty per cent of their forests include trees damaged in varying ways, from disrupted growth, through needle discolouration and drop to actual death of the trees.

Wherever we live, we are all affected by, or contribute to, pollution in one way or another. The pollution problem can no longer be ignored. Burning fossil fuels, poisonous fumes that cars pump into the atmosphere, cutting down tropical rain forests and technological changes in farming and industry are only some of the human activities which have led to the release and increase of the so-called greenhouse gases.

For example, each year as much as two and a half billion tons of carbon dioxide are released from burning forests, adding to emissions from fossil fuels. As this gas traps the sun's heat in the atmosphere, scientists fear that the earth may grow warmer, melting polar ice and flooding low-lying coastal regions.

Sadly, 20,000 square kilometres of rain forest, largely in South and Central America, are cleared annually to create grazing land for beef cattle. The majority of this meat is exported to the United States for fast-food burger eaters. One day's worth of 'rain-forest burgers', placed side by side, would stretch from Nicaragua to New York, then back to the hungry people of Costa Rica.

Pollution is a dreadful problem but we are learning more about its extent, causes and dangers. One thing is obvious: we can no longer afford to ignore the problem. Time is running out for us. Action is required. Such action is made more urgent by the fact that this is God's world. 'The earth is the Lord's,' the Bible declares, 'and everything in it...' (Ps. 24:1). Furthermore, our Creator-God has given us responsibilities to care for his world (Gen. 1:28-30).

Moral pollution

But that is not the sum total of the problem by any means. One reason is that pollution extends beyond environmental issues and the world of nature. There is also the ugly reality of moral pollution affecting all humans. Our contemporary, secular world rarely acknowledges or discusses this aspect of pollution but the Bible gives great prominence to it. In fact, it is sin and moral pollution that largely cause and aggravate environmental pollution.

The fact of moral pollution was brought home again to me some time ago. News programmes reported that a twenty-seven-year-old man had been ordered by a London court to serve five life sentences. The convicted man had murdered a taxi-driver who had disturbed him ransacking his home and he had also stabbed to death a woman he knew. Only a week later he had stabbed and killed a police sergeant, then hours later attacked two police officers when they tried to question him and an accomplice. Sentencing him, the judge said that the man had shown himself to be 'quite pitiless, without any vestige of remorse' for his victims and their families. The judge added that the prisoner was 'evil through and through'. In other words, he was morally polluted.

Perhaps you feel relieved at this point. After all, you have not killed anyone. Perhaps you have never committed a serious crime at all. On the contrary, you may regard yourself as a good person, respectable, kind and harmless. Others, too, may think the same about you. As far as you are concerned, therefore, the judge's words do not apply to you. And this is a commonly held view. Only notorious criminals, people argue, are polluted morally. The rest of us are pretty good. Well, pause and consider what God says about us in the Bible.

Are we basically good? Is sin or evil something which only criminals and freaks are capable of committing? What is the real truth about ourselves?

We all inherit a sinful nature

As we saw in the last chapter, the Bible teaches that 'Sin entered the world through one man', that is, Adam (Rom. 5:12). A perfect, harmonious world was suddenly shattered by Adam's disobedience to the command of God. Remember, too, that Adam sinned both as an individual and as a representative of mankind, so that he plunged the whole of humanity into sin with all its tragic consequences. Now one of these consequences was the moral pollution of all humans. Allow me to explain.

Adam could only pass on to his descendants a polluted, sinful human nature. From birth, therefore, our human nature is polluted by sin, and we inherit this sin from Adam. 'Surely,' confessed David, 'I was sinful at birth, sinful from the time my mother conceived me' (Ps. 51:5). Acknowledging this fact, Job asked, 'Who can bring what is pure from the impure? No one!' was his immediate reply (Job 14:4). 'Like the rest,' the apostle Paul writes, 'we were by nature objects of wrath' (Eph. 2:3). The words 'by nature' here are crucial. Our sinful condition is not something we pick up later in life, nor is it the result of bad company, unwise choices, poor education or unfortunate circumstances. A child does not need to be trained to disobey; rather, it is something each child does naturally. It is so natural for children to be selfish and disobedient that parents have no choice but to teach and discipline them to obey. And the reason for this natural bias towards evil is that we are all born with a sinful, polluted nature; it is what theologians call 'original sin'. From Adam, we all inherit a sinful nature.

Some time ago, a small group of technicians in a hospital pathology laboratory were arguing among themselves on this subject. At a critical point in the argument, the consultant pathologist walked in and listened briefly to the discussion. As a Christian, he interjected with the words: 'It is a matter of observation, and not argument, that children are born with a bias to sin and a moral nature that is polluted.' He was right. No one can say, 'I am clean and without sin' (Prov. 20:9). The point is repeated several times in the Bible: 'There is no one righteous, not even one ... for all have sinned and fall short of the glory of God' (Rom. 3:10,23). Nor are there any exceptions; it is true of us all.

The extent of moral pollution

There is even more to say about moral pollution. Sin actually extends to all areas of our lives. Whether it is behaviour, words, thoughts, or motives and desires, the Bible declares that sin has extended its influence to all these areas. We are sinful 'through and through'. However, this must not be misunderstood. It does not mean that we all indulge in all forms of sin. That is just not true. Many of us, for example, are horrified to hear of a gunman entering a family house in Northern Ireland and shooting the father at close range in front of his three young children. Nor would many of us want to batter our wives, abuse our children or rape and attack other individuals. In fact, we feel very angry that people do these dreadful things.

We must go even further in removing possible misunderstandings. Being sinful 'through and through' does not prevent us from doing good things. An obvious example is a father who cares lovingly for his wife and children, or a person who helps an old lady who has fallen on the pavement. Or think of a mother who donates her kidney for her child in life-saving kidney transplant surgery. An older man in my home area goes shopping for several sick and aged folk who are housebound. He also calls regularly to see that they are comfortable, and all this is done without payment. A great deal of civil good is also undertaken by individuals who are concerned for the welfare of the community. However, in relation to God even these 'good' actions are defective. In many cases, for example, they are not motivated by the glory of God, nor are they prompted by God's love. 'And without faith it is impossible to please God' (Heb. 11:6).

What does it mean, therefore, when the Bible teaches we are sinful 'through and through'? First of all, it means that *the pollution of sin extends to each part of our nature*. Obviously I can both say and do things which are wrong. Although small, the tongue is capable of lying, criticizing, swearing and expressing anger or hatred. Sin, therefore, extends to our talking. And there is no limit to the sins we commit in our daily actions. But there is more. Our minds are also polluted by sin. Would you like your closest relative or friend to know all the thoughts you think in your mind? Probably not. You may appear nice with folk and smile in conversation with them but in your thoughts you may dislike and even hate them. That is also sin. And this is not just my opinion. None other than the Lord Jesus Christ himself affirms it. Read what he says in

Matthew 5:21-22: 'You have heard that it was said to the people long ago, "Do not murder..." But I tell you that anyone who is angry ... will be subject to judgement.' The same is true of adultery. 'Anyone,' declared Jesus, 'who looks at a woman lustfully has already committed adultery with her in his heart' (Matt. 5:28).

Secondly, we are sinful 'through and through' because *there is no spiritual good in us*. In other words, we cannot do anything which matches up to the perfect standards of God's holy law. Our very best actions are hopelessly defective, so it is impossible for us to get God's approval. Nor can we alter the bias in our nature towards self and sin. Make no mistake about it, we are all deeply biased towards sin. Have you noticed how sad childhood experiences can affect and bias some children in their adult behaviour?

Vincent Van Gogh, whose painting of sunflowers held the world record price of £25 million, died in 1892. Van Gogh was a replacement child for a still-born son but sadly he was denied the love of his mother. This fact laid the foundation for depression and aggravated his later failures.

Similarly, Sheila Scott had a turbulent childhood because her mother deserted the family when she was only three years of age. She was affected deeply by this and it was a major factor in disposing her towards mental illness and drugs. Only at the age of thirty-six did she overcome these problems sufficiently to become a pioneering aviator who broke more than a hundred light-aircraft records.

The point I am making is this: we have all been biased, not in the direction of depression or drugs like Van Gogh and Scott, but in the direction of sin. Although the problem started with Adam yet it does not stop there. For we also choose to sin ourselves. It is our decision to sin and we cannot shift the blame on to anyone else but ourselves. We are all personally guilty.

We are off course

Not so long ago, a fishmonger had a fifteen-stone shark in his shop, which he intended to cut up and sell. Trawler-men believe the six-foot-long porbeagle was basking in the warm waters off the African coast when freak winter storms turned it off course and it was eventually caught off the south coast of Britain. What has this story got to do with us? Well, I am using the story as an illustration of the way in which we have all gone 'off course' as humans.

Put it this way. The Bible makes it clear that before he sinned, Adam was on course. That means he was fulfilling the purpose set for his life by God. And what was that purpose? Essentially it was to obey and please God. This is the reason why God created Adam and all subsequent human beings: 'Thou hast created all things, and for thy pleasure they are and were created' (Rev. 4:11, AV). There is no higher purpose in life than this: 'All things were created by him [Jesus Christ] and for him' (Col. 1:16). Before he sinned, Adam's greatest pleasure was to obey God. His whole life centred around God. All that he thought, desired, said and did honoured God. To put it another way, Adam did not live for business, money, sex, sport or fame. Not at all. Although he was happily married, the most important person in his life was God. Does that sound boring, a miserable existence? By no means, for Adam was exceptionally happy. His pleasure was in knowing, enjoying and serving God. And there is no pleasure or relationship to compare with it. Adam was on course. He was travelling on the main road appointed by God.

Suddenly, however, there was a crash and the world's greatest tragedy occurred. We usually call it 'the Fall'. Adam and Eve listened to the devil, turned off God's road and walked onto the dark and dangerous road of sin, rebellion, selfishness, pain and misery. The tragic crash is described in Genesis chapter 3. Since then, we have all been 'off course' and live as if God does not matter or even exist. We desperately need to be rescued.

Does it really matter that we are off course and lost? What has God got to do with the world and with my life? These questions will be answered in the next few chapters.

18.
God

Who is God? What is God like? One wrong answer to these important questions is provided by the American actress Shirley MacLaine. Some years ago she stood, with a large group of people, on the shore of the Pacific Ocean claiming for herself, 'I am God. I am that I am.' She meant it, too; she was not joking or acting. Not at all. For Christians, her claim is blasphemous but for Shirley MacLaine and her followers it is central to New Age teaching. Because New Age ideas are popular at present, it will be helpful to say a little more about them before we explain what the Bible correctly says about God.

The background to the New Age movement

Fashionable in the West since the late 1960s, New Age teaching is a Western adaptation of Eastern mysticism. And its history is interesting. The 1960s were a turbulent and radical decade in many ways. Politically, there was the Cuban crisis, followed by the horrors of Vietnam, the Cold War and the imminent threat of a world nuclear war. Socially, post-war babies entered the colleges as teenagers reacting against the restraints of the establishment, family and church. They marched for freedom and peace while strikes occurred frequently within industry.

Religiously, churches were in serious decline and congregations dwindled. Even worse, many had abandoned the message of the Bible. New radical ideas became the vogue. In 1963, for example, John Robinson, who at the time was Bishop of Woolwich, published a popular rehash of the views of some critical theologians in his *Honest to God*. One and a half million copies of the book, which represented a denial of biblical teaching, were sold within a few months. There was even worse to come. A group of theologians talked about the death of God. For them, God had died in nineteenth-century European and American thought and literature. Even God was regarded by them as being subject to the same changes of growth and decay as humans; God had accepted self-annihilation.

No wonder that the church was seen by the majority of people to be irrelevant and devoid of a message. In this vacuum, people became restless, disillusioned and groped for satisfying answers. Increasing numbers turned to drugs, but it was the Beatles, especially George Harrison, who discovered Eastern mysticism. In February 1967, Harrison made his first contact with the Maharishi Mahesh Yogi in India. His response was positive. Referring to the 'spiritual' side of Indian music, he announced to the world that 'Now it is the only reason for living... Eastern religion taught me that the ideal is to become one with God through meditation and yoga.' A new generation of young people in the West were gradually enticed into the world of Eastern mysticism.

Monism

What do New Age-ers believe? We are concerned in this chapter with God, so we draw attention to two distinctive New

Age theories which relate to their view of God. One theory is monism. Perhaps the word does not convey anything to you. Put simply, it means that everything in the world is one; we are all fragments of the great cosmic consciousness and thereby possess innate divinity. Allow me to illustrate the absurdity of monism. According to this concept, there is no difference, for example, between a tree and a human. Any differences you perceive are due to your own ignorance, for actually trees and humans are all one. That is why some New Age followers stand by a tree; they meditate, they 'feel' for the tree, sometimes they embrace the tree in an attempt to enter into union with it.

Similarly, monism claims, there is no difference between dogs and humans. Is this not taking it too far? In a large New Age centre in Pasadena, California, the expensive courses which are on offer all aim to achieve oneness with dogs! If you go there for a day or a week, you must get down on your hands and knees and try to communicate with a dog without talking!

In a small New Age community in Findhorn, Scotland, all the kitchen utensils have labels describing them as 'metal' or 'wooden beings'. Again, the theory is that there is no difference between inanimate objects such as a spoon, fork or even a car and ourselves! Such is the central tenet of New Age thinking, namely, monism.

Pantheism

There is, however, another theory which is closely related to monism and equally important to New Age thinking, namely, pantheism. By this is meant the belief that everything which exists, including humans, makes up God; in other words, the whole world and all that is in it is actually God. Whether cows, trees, birds, insects or humans, all are equally divine and form an essential part of God and his characteristics. Humans, then, have an unlimited potential of divinity which they need to realize by various methods of meditation. No wonder that Shirley MacLaine declared, 'I am God. I am that I am.' She actually imagines that to be true.

But what is the real truth? Who is God? And what is he like? These are important questions but we can no longer take the answers for granted. There is confusion and ignorance today concerning the true God. Not only that, people have twisted and changed the idea of God in order to suit themselves. They have created their own kind of God. By contrast, consider some of the facts that God gives in the Bible about himself. There are four facts, in particular, which are relevant to our theme in this chapter.

God is independent

First of all, God is independent of us and the world. The Bible declares that God is 'high and exalted' (Isa. 6:1), that is, he is apart from us, separate and glorious. He is not a mere super-man. Nor is he the sum-total and aggregate of all that exists in the world. Rather, he is 'the High and Lofty One who inhabits eternity' (Isa. 57:15, NKJV). He exists outside of us and apart from us. To put it in another way, God is independent in his nature and essence. His nature is not fused, mixed or merged with the world. No, God exists by himself and he does not depend on anything or anyone else for his well-being or survival. This is true also of all that God does. He created the world on his own, but even before the world was created, God existed as the one, solitary and eternal God. He also preserves and governs the world as he pleases and again he does so without help or advice from anyone outside the Godhead. While all that God created remains completely dependent on him, God himself continues to be independent of his creation. Consider, for example, how the Bible distinguishes between God and the world which he made:

> He sits enthroned above the circle of the earth,
>   and its people are like grasshoppers.
> He stretches out the heavens like a canopy,
>   and spreads them out like a tent to live in...
>
> 'To whom will you compare me?
>   Or who is my equal?' says the Holy One.
> Lift your eyes and look to the heavens;
>   Who created all these?
> He who brings out the starry host one by one,
>   and calls them each by name.
> Because of his great power and mighty strength,
>   not one of them is missing
>
> (Isa. 40:22, 25-26).

Trees, then, are not divine and they do not participate in God's nature. Nor do cows, dogs or other animals share in the divine nature. New Age theories about God are wrong. There is only one God and he exists independently of people, animals and nature. This independent, transcendent and wholly other God is glorious but awesome. And it matters to him how we live. To be 'off course' in our lives means danger and ultimate disaster.

God is infinite

Secondly, God is free from all human limitations. In other words, he is infinite. As humans we are limited in all kinds of ways. We can only be in one place at a time. However clever people become, their knowledge always remains limited. Nor do humans have the ability to achieve all that they want. Human lives are bounded by space and divided into days, weeks, months and years.

By contrast, God is infinite; he has none of our limitations at all. His knowledge is complete and there is nothing at all which he does not know. He has no need to learn or use reference books to gain knowledge; as God he knows everything. God also has the power to do all that he desires and plans. There is no failure or frustration with God. Neither is his nature limited in terms of time or decay. He is eternal and unchanging. 'I the Lord,' he affirms, 'do not change' (Mal. 3:6). Remember also that 'God is spirit' (John 4:24) and has no body like humans and animals. He is 'the King eternal, immortal, invisible, the only God' (1 Tim. 1:17) and 'lives in unapproachable light, whom no one has seen or can see' (1 Tim. 6:16). It is foolish, therefore, for New Age-ers to claim that humans, animals, trees and the whole creation constitute God. It is just not true, for God is spirit and unseen.

God's relationship with his creation

Thirdly, while being independent and infinite, God nevertheless chooses to have a close relationship with the world he made. As we have seen, this relationship is not a necessary one, for God exists apart from the world. On the other hand, God freely enters into different kinds of relationships with his creation and those living in it.

For example, he cares for and preserves the world he made. He is not like the clockmaker who makes a clock, sells it and forgets all about it afterwards. Far from it. By Christ, 'All things were created ... and in him all things hold together' (Col. 1:16,17). He is 'sustaining all things by his powerful word' (Heb. 1:3).

Then again, though God transcends space his presence is everywhere. This is what we mean when we speak of God being omnipresent. God is near to us all, wherever we are, yet distinct from us. Wherever you go in the universe, God is there and there is no escape from him. Admittedly, 'The heavens, even the highest heaven, cannot contain' God (1 Kings 8:27), yet he is also a God who is near and whose presence is everywhere.

'Am I only a God nearby,'

declares the Lord,

'and not a God far away?
Can anyone hide in secret places
    so that I cannot see him?'

declares the Lord.

'Do not I fill heaven and earth?'

declares the Lord
(Jer. 23:23-24).

David, the psalmist, knew there was no possibility of hiding from God's presence:

Where can I go from your Spirit?
    Where can I flee from your presence?
If I go up to the heavens, you are there;
    if I make my bed in the depths, you are there.
If I rise on the wings of the dawn,
    if I settle on the far side of the sea,
even there your hand will guide me,
    your right hand will hold me fast

(Ps. 139:7-10).

Yes, God is present everywhere. For those who trust in the Lord Jesus Christ, God is present with them in a special way. In fact the relationship between them and the Lord is an intimate and spiritual one. Christ actually lives in Christians by the Holy Spirit, yet always remains distinct even from them.

Man, a unique creation of God

Finally, the Bible informs us that humans are a unique creation of God. What am I? Am I God, as Shirley Maclaine claims? No, we are certainly not God. The Bible is emphatic on this point. On the other hand, man is special, for he has been made in the likeness, or image, of God. On the sixth day of creation, God paused between two creative acts and within the Holy Trinity took counsel before creating man: 'Let us make man in our image, in our likeness...' (Gen. 1:26). This illustrates how unique we are as humans in God's creation.

Remember, too, that God created fish, birds, animals, etc., 'according to their kinds' (Gen. 1:21), that is, in a way typical and exclusive to themselves only. In contrast, man was created in God's likeness. We resemble animals in some respects, for example in needing food and rest. Animals and humans also have in common the senses of hearing, seeing, smelling, tasting and feeling. Nevertheless, there is an essential difference between ourselves and animals. Man, unlike the animals, is God-related; he is made in the image of God.

What does it mean to be created 'in God's image'?

You may have a question in your mind at this point: namely, what does it mean to say that we have been made in God's image? There are several things to bear in mind in understanding the meaning of this expression.

Firstly, just as God has personality — a mind, will and the power to love and hate — so man has these characteristics of personality.

God also has a moral nature. He hates sin and loves what is pure. As humans, we have been given a moral nature by God and, despite sin, have a continuing sense of right and wrong.

In addition, God is spirit and he made humans, and only humans, with a spiritual dimension to their lives. We are not a mere composition of chemicals, or just physical bodies. Again, only God is immortal, yet when God created us he created us for an eternal destiny. Death is not the end of our existence, as it is for animals; we shall live eternally after death in either heaven or hell.

We are now in a better position to understand some of the Bible's answers to our questions about human nature and existence. What am I? I am a person created by God and radically different from the rest of creation. God's image is upon me but I am not, and never can be, God. New Age teaching is, therefore, condemned by the Bible, as is also Mormonism. The latter teaches that God is Adam; in other words, God was once a human being like ourselves who progressed to become an exalted being. Mormons claim that men and women who 'seal' their marriages in a Mormon temple become 'gods', while unmarried people only become angels after death. No, there is only one God. 'Besides him there is no other' (Deut. 4:35). We are neither divine now, as New Age-ers claim, nor will we become divine in the future, as Mormons teach. God is eternally and essentially different and separate from his creation, yet there are, as we have seen, important points of resemblance between God and humans.

God's purpose for our lives

Is there a purpose for our lives? Yes, there is, and it is an important, satisfying one. God's purpose for us is that we should enjoy, obey and glorify him. Not even the happiest experiences in life can be compared with this. Meeting and marrying a person you love is deeply satisfying. Holding your own baby is thrilling. Passing an examination brings a sense of achievement. However, it is only when we know and obey God that we realize this ultimate joy and purpose in our lives.

It matters that we are sinful and 'off course' because God is holy and we are obliged to obey him. This will become clearer in the following chapters.

19.
Sin

It matters, then, how we live. And sin is a major problem. As we have seen, sin is a problem because of what God is like, and we shall return to this theme shortly, in chapters 21 and 22. However, sin is also a problem because of the damage it causes in people's lives and in society generally. Sin creates havoc, pain, sadness and disaster.

The headlines in my newspaper as I write this make sad reading: 'Knife-wielding son burgled mother's home,' threatening as well as frightening her; 'Two held after bus-stop killing,' in which an eighteen-year-old male was stabbed to death by a gang of white youths while waiting for a bus in London. On the same page were the headlines, '"Joy-ride" killer faces stiff sentence,' and 'OAP conned'. The 'joy-ride' killer was a drunken motorcyclist who ran over and killed a policeman in the Midlands, whereas the 'con-man', claiming to be a plumber concerned about a water leak, gained access to the house of a ninety-year-old woman in North Wales and stole more than £600. A report headed, 'Undercover police in drug stake-out,' informs me of a massive six-million-pounds international drugs racket discovered by police in my home area. A distressing headline declares that a 'Chiropodist had sex with girl, 13.' On the next page I am reminded of the fighting in the former Yugoslavia and the atrocities being committed there: 'Serbs attack town in defiance of UN.' The town is the Muslim enclave of Zepa, to which the United Nations has given the status of a UN 'safe area'. 40,000 civilians and refugees are trapped there, but over 500 people have been killed already. My attention is also drawn to another headline: 'No end to Germany's scandals.' Within a year, three German government ministers have resigned, the latest because of alleged misuse of public funds.

'What has all this got to do with me?'

There are numerous other headlines I could quote from the newspaper, which all illustrate the havoc and suffering caused by human sin. And the story is the same, day by day. You may be shocked to read what some people do; perhaps the news also saddens and angers you. 'I have not killed or robbed anyone,' you may add, 'nor have I been immoral or involved myself in a drugs racket.' What you are saying about yourself and others may be true; many of us are law-abiding and respectable in the way we live. Perhaps, however, you feel confused on the point. 'How can I be "off course" and sinful,' you ask, 'if I have never done any of the bad things referred to in the newspaper headlines? After all, I am not a criminal.' The question is an important one and deserves our attention for the rest of the chapter.

Missing God's purpose for us

Although we may not ourselves have been guilty of stealing or murdering, yet the Bible declares that we 'all have sinned and fall short of the glory of God' (Rom. 3:23). There is not a single human person anywhere in the world who has not sinned:

'There is no one righteous, not even one' (Rom. 3:10). Perhaps you still cannot understand how you yourself can be called a sinner. Well, it is important to understand what sin is, so we shall consider some of the words used in the Bible to describe sin.

One word frequently used in the Bible to describe sin means 'to miss'. The word applies to us in two related ways.

First of all, it literally means that we have missed *something*; that is, we have failed to achieve the purpose of God for our lives. God's purpose in creating us is that we should love, obey and glorify him all the time. There is no greater reason for living than this. Sin, however, means that we have missed this great purpose for our lives and are content to live for lesser things, whether people, money, pleasure, sport or sex, etc.

A deliberate choice

The Bible makes it clear that we have missed God's purpose by choice and not merely by accident or ignorance. For example, when I go to a large town or city for the first time and have to find my own way by car to a certain house, church or college I am usually given directions how to reach my destination. I confess that there have been occasions when I have lost my way because I found it extremely difficult to follow the directions. Consequently, I took a wrong turning, or went into the wrong traffic lane, which took me off my intended route. But it was not my intention to get lost. I definitely did not look for an opportunity to take an alternative route. No, I lost my way through ignorance; that is, I was not familiar with the area. But this is not true of us in relation to God. We wilfully choose to miss God's purpose for our lives and prefer to live a selfish, sinful life rather than obey and please God. This is something deliberate on our part. Three times in Romans 1:18-32 the apostle Paul emphasizes this aspect of the deliberate nature of human sin. We 'suppress the truth' (v. 18), that is, the truth that God exists, that he is eternal and powerful, that he created the world and that we are duty bound to honour him.

The voice of conscience

Even if we choose to believe that God does not exist and reject his rules for our lives, yet, through our consciences, the 'truth' continues to trouble and warn us. We may try hard to silence or weaken the voice of conscience in all kinds of ways. One way is to argue against God and creation. Others try to explain away conscience in terms of upbringing, while some endeavour to drown its message by even more sin and drunkenness, or a busy working life. Conscience, however, is God's voice inside us registering the fact of God's existence and our corresponding duty to obey him. Our problem, then, is not ignorance but our deliberate rejection of the truth because we prefer to go in an entirely different direction.

This is underlined again in verse 28 of Romans 1, where we are told that people do 'not think it worth while to retain the knowledge of God'. While it is true that we all miss the mark of God's purpose for our lives, we are told here that we do not even try to achieve it. We prefer to live as if God does not exist and pretend there is no divine purpose which we are obliged to fulfil.

Later, in verse 32, the apostle Paul declares that we 'continue to do these very things' which God forbids. And, even worse, we 'also approve of those who practise them'. As usual, the Bible is perfectly correct in what it says about us here. We do persist in sinning, although it may prove costly in terms of losing our reputation, our job, our health, or even our family. There is more, too. We approve of others who do the same things in flouting God's standards. Pleasure is found in talking and joking about such sins; instead of shame, there is boasting and laughter. Make no mistake about it, sin is a deliberate missing of God's purpose for our lives and we are all guilty.

Missing the mark

Secondly, the word 'miss' has the related meaning of missing the mark. The picture now is that of a marksman who aims for a target with his gun but misses. Or it may be a young person who fails an examination. He needs fifty per cent to obtain a pass but only succeeds in getting forty-five per cent. He fails because his marks are below the required standard. This idea is conveyed in Romans 3:23 in the words: 'and fall short of the glory of God'. Sin means we have missed the mark of God's perfection and fallen well below the standards God has set for our lives. These standards are set out for us clearly in God's law, such as the Ten Commandments in Exodus 20. Not one of us has kept these commands as God requires. We have sinned by failing to reach the standard of God's holy laws.

Transgression

Another word the Bible uses for sin means lawlessness, the transgression and breaking of the law. 'Everyone who sins breaks the law; in fact, sin is lawlessness' (1 John 3:4). Basically, the word 'to transgress' means to cross over a boundary into a prohibited area. It may be the boundary of a country which someone crosses illegally. His motive may be to spy or rob. Whatever the motive, the law is broken. The person is rebelling against the lawful government of that country. He is a rebel and law-breaker.

Here is a picture of our attitude towards God. By nature, we are law-breakers, transgressing not against a country but against God, his laws and his Word. Sin disposes us to do what God prohibits. This note of disobedience is dominant in Romans 5:12-19.

Do you see yourself as a law-breaker before God — yes, you? In failing to love God and your neighbours, in lying and stealing, in not giving Sundays to the worship and service of God, or by using the name of God lightly in conversation or as a swear word — in any or all of these ways, you have broken God's laws. And there are other laws, too, which you have broken.

Rebellion

Linked with disobedience and the breaking of God's laws is the idea of sin as rebellion against God. The sinner is a rebel who refuses to obey God. He prefers to oppose God and please himself. 'Why should I listen to God?' he asks. 'I'll do as I please and no one, not even God, will order me what to do.' This is the language of rebellion and defiance. In rebellion man breaks the laws of God. He refuses to love God, he will not keep Sunday special, nor will he respect and help his parents. Rather, he insists on doing the opposite of what God commands.

Such rebellion is sin, for it is our duty to obey God all the time. Why must we obey God? One reason is because we stand as humans in a creature-Creator relationship to God. As Creator-God, he has the authority to command us how to live and we are all under the authority of God, whether we like it or not. He is God. He also rules the world he made and we are all obliged to obey him.

A debt

'Debt' is another word the Bible uses to describe sin. In a pattern prayer given to the disciples, the Lord Jesus taught them to pray: 'Forgive us our debts, as we also have forgiven our debtors' (Matt. 6:12). In what sense is sin a debt? This expression does not mean, of course, that we owe sin to God. Nor does it mean that we have a debt of money owing to God. Rather, the word refers to the debt of obedience we all owe to God. Perfect obedience is what God demands from us. We are under a binding obligation to obey God completely in all things. Sadly, not one of us is able to pay God this debt of obedience, a debt which is owing to him from each human person in the world. Sin is in that sense a debt.

Iniquity

The Bible also speaks of sin as 'iniquity' (Job 6:29,30, AV; Ps. 37:1, AV). This word means bending or changing the shape of something. For example, a book may be bent after being mishandled, or the word can be used to describe the action of a blacksmith when, after putting a piece of iron into the fire, he hammers it into a different shape. Sometimes a person suffering from rheumatoid arthritis will find that his or her fingers become twisted out of shape and extremely painful. In a similar way, sin is something which distorts and twists our lives. While God commands us to live a holy life centred around himself, sin has changed the pattern of our life so that we actually turn our backs on God and break his laws. Sin means, then, that our lives are not the right shape. We need to be remade and turned back to God.

Are we really 'off course'? Can we properly be called sinners if we have never committed a major crime? The answer is yes. To miss God's purpose and standard for our lives is sin. Disobedience is sin, and so is rebellion. The debt of obedience which we are unable to pay God is also sin. Remember, too, that sin has changed our lives for the worse. Now this is true of us all; there is not one human person who is without sin. Does it matter? That is the theme of the next chapter.

20.
Guilty!

A twenty-four-year-old nurse was found guilty of murdering four children she was supposed to be looking after in hospital. One nine-week-old premature twin was admitted to the hospital with a stomach upset. Three days later, after having been fed by the nurse, the child was allowed to go home. However, that evening she began screaming in pain, had convulsions and eventually stopped breathing. Although taken back to hospital, the child died and later analysis found that her blood contained a very high level of insulin. Another child was admitted at the same time to the hospital with chronic asthma. She was found to have turned dark blue and stopped breathing after being left alone with the nurse. This child died, too, and a post-mortem examination found the level of potassium in her blood was so high that it was off the scale of hospital equipment. Later dubbed as the 'Angel of Death', the nurse was found guilty of killing four children.

In what was described by some as the 'trial of the century', the self-styled 'world's richest man' (Adanan Koshiggi) and, until the late eighties, the 'globe's biggest spender' (Imelda Marcos) were charged in 1990 with stealing 190 million pounds from the people of the Philippines and several American banks. The prosecution had no doubt about it; they were guilty.

In Cambodia, by the late 1970s, more than one and a half million people had been killed in the country during Pol Pot's reign of terror. Cambodia lost most of a generation and is now dominated by women and children. Whole sections of the community were massacred. The well-educated were slaughtered, including the majority of medical doctors, solicitors, teachers and those with administrative skills. People were even killed for wearing glasses, or simply for living too close to the Vietnamese border, where they might act as collaborators. The whole infrastructure of the society was destroyed. All this devastation was inflicted on the country by Pol Pot in his cruel reign which lasted for only four years. There are ominous signs that Pol Pot is seeking to recapture Cambodia again. Is he guilty? Certainly, and guilty of the most dreadful, inhuman atrocities. The conditions were a nightmare and 'Bombs equal to five Hiroshimas fell on Cambodia.'

The relevance for us

What has all this got to do with us? Well, it is relevant if only for purposes of information and interest. We dare not be indifferent to what is happening to individuals and nations. But these examples are relevant for another reason, too. Pause for a moment to consider what the terms 'guilt' and 'guilty' mean. Dictionaries define the noun 'guilt' as 'punishable conduct: the state of having broken a law'. It is further defined as a 'crime' and 'wickedness'. The adjective 'guilty' describes people who are 'justly chargeable with a crime', that is, breaking the law of a country. Such persons deserve punishment because they are responsible for breaking the law. The nurse, therefore, who was guilty of four child murders deserved to be sentenced to imprisonment for a lengthy period of time. She was guilty.

Now this, in principle, is what the Bible says about men and women everywhere. We have all sinned against God. In the last chapter, we saw that our sin involves missing the purpose and standard of God and there is also deliberate disobedience on our part in breaking God's laws. Disobedience involves rebellion against God. And that is not all. We have a permanent obligation to obey our Creator-God completely in all things and at all times. No one, however, is able to pay this debt of obedience to God, so sin involves a debt. This means that we are guilty people because of the sins that we have committed and that we are unable to remove or change. That is the message of the apostle Paul in Romans 3:19-20: '... so that every mouth may be silenced and the whole world held accountable to God'. It is the law of God which condemns us, the very same law which we break continually in our lives. There is no excuse. And we have no defence that will bear the scrutiny of God the Judge. We have no way of avoiding our guilt either.

The apostle James underlines the same principle but adds: 'For whoever keeps the whole law and yet stumbles at just one point is guilty of breaking all of it' (James 2:10). Failure to keep God's law in only one detail makes us guilty. There is no doubt about it. We all deserve God's condemnation and punishment; that is what guilt means for us in our relationship to God. To sin against God is an extremely serious matter.

An important distinction

A distinction needs to be made at this point in order to avoid confusion. It concerns guilt as a fact and guilt as something which we feel and acknowledge. For example, a man may be guilty of stealing tools from his factory, but for various reasons may not feel guilty about it. He may justify his actions in all kinds of ways, by referring to his low wages, his selfish boss or the trivial nature of the things he takes. If you press the fact of his guilt, he may only laugh and regard you as a fool for being narrow and old-fashioned. The truth is that the man does not acknowledge his guilt although he is actually guilty of stealing from his employer. By contrast, a man may lose his temper with his wife, say all kinds of cruel things about her and even threaten to end the relationship. Several hours later, after reflecting on the outburst, he may begin to feel guilty. Because of his sense of guilt he acknowledges to his wife that he has done wrong and seeks forgiveness. While the story may not always have a happy ending, his awareness of guilt is a major step in seeking reconciliation and forgiveness.

Two historical examples will illustrate the distinction further. In December 1989, some of the surviving USA atombombers travelled to Hiroshima in virtual secrecy to see the city they reduced to ashes in 1945. But it was not a sense of guilt which made them return to Hiroshima. Not at all. One of the air crew, General Charles 'Chuck' Sweeney, was insistent: 'The world has a solemn duty to remember what we did — because what we did was to keep the peace, and make it possible for Communism to be dismantled in Central Europe.' There were no acts of contrition on the part of the air crew. The BBC's *Inside Story* documentary series filmed the visit of these veterans to Hiroshima; it was shown on television in the United Kingdom in April 1990 under the title, *Return to Hiroshima*. The TV commentary includes the words: 'The veterans have no time for critics of their wartime action — and they reject those who say that what they did was wrong and that the atomic bomb should never have been used. They say that 160,000 deaths by blast, fire and irradiation and the total destruction of Hiroshima itself were fully justified because it led to the end of the war and victory for the Allies. And to this day each one of them believes that.' I am not taking sides concerning the rightness or wrongness of their action. All I want you to notice is their refusal to acknowledge they had done wrong; for them, their action was justified.

Consider a very different example. In April 1990 the Polish people received an acknowledgement from the Russian leaders that they, and not the Nazis, had been responsible for the killing of nearly 15,000 Polish army officers in 1940. The officers were from the part of Poland occupied by Soviet forces under a secret Soviet-German agreement at the start of World War II. They were transported eastwards and then disappeared. About 4,000 bodies were discovered at Katyn, near Smolensk but the whereabouts of the rest are still unknown. On 13 April 1990, the Tass news agency said that the Russian government expressed its deepest regrets over the incident and that it was one of the worst Stalinist crimes. The British Katyn Association welcomed 'the inexcusably belated admission of Soviet guilt'.

What this means for our relationship to God

We need now to apply the above distinction between the fact of guilt and the acknowledgement of guilt to ourselves and our relationship to God. While 'All have sinned and fall short of the glory of God' (Rom. 3:23), not many people are prepared to acknowledge their personal sin and guilt. They may actually insist, like the USA atom-bomb pilots, that what they do is right. 'After all,' they may say, 'we are quite good people, respectable, law-abiding and supportive of our families. Don't call us sinners!' Do you think like this? Is this your honest view of yourself?

If so, consider the way in which God brings sinners to face up to their guilt and sinfulness. God's method is to use his law. 'Through the law', Paul reminds us, 'we become conscious of sin' (Rom. 3:20). The law has been given to us in order to show us the fact of our sin. This is an important function of God's law; it drives home to us the fact that we have disobeyed and broken the commands of God. However, it does not stop there: '… through the commandment,' adds Paul, 'sin might become utterly sinful' (Rom. 7:13). In other words, the law is also given to us in order to show how wicked sin really is. That is why when a person sees the significance of the law of God he then begins to see his own wickedness and guilt before God. Frederick Whitefield expressed it well in his hymn:

> I need thee, precious Jesus!
> For I am full of sin;
> My soul is dark and guilty,
> My heart is dead within;
> I need the cleansing fountain,
> Where I can always flee,
> The blood of Christ most precious,
> The sinner's perfect plea.

It is the law of God that enables a person to see and say such things. This sense of guilt is accompanied by a growing conviction that it is impossible to save oneself. The standard required by God, as expressed in the law, is now seen in terms of a mountain which is insurmountable. A sense of helplessness, guilt and danger grips the individual. In this way, God's law 'was put in charge to lead us to Christ' (Gal. 3:24). That is why Charles Wesley wrote the famous lines of his hymn:

> Other refuge have I none;
> Hangs my helpless soul on thee.

In a later verse of the same hymn, he declares:

Just and holy is thy name,
I am all unrighteousness;
False and full of sin I am,
Thou art full of truth and grace.

Where do you stand? Yes, you are guilty and sinful. But do you own up to it? Are you prepared to make a 'belated admission' of guilt like the Russians over the Katyn atrocity? Or do you still insist, like the American pilots, that you have done nothing wrong? Well, read on, for in the next chapter we shall see what it means to say that God is holy. Unless you grasp the fact of your sin and the holy character of God you will not appreciate or see the need of Christ's sacrifice on the cross.

21.
God — holy and angry

He was a young man with a promising career in the service of the King of Judah. His name was Isaiah. It was about 740 B.C. and the future appeared bleak for Isaiah's nation. One reason was that his king, Uzziah, had just died. Feeling somewhat fearful and sad, the young man went to the nearby temple in Jerusalem to worship God. It was an ordinary service and no one seems to have expected anything unusual to happen. Suddenly, however, it was all different, at least for Isaiah. While he worshipped in the temple, God appeared to him in a vision. It was overwhelming and shattering. He would never be the same again. His career, too, was changed. Instead of his remaining a statesman for the rest of his life, God called him to be a preacher.

A breathtaking experience

What happened? Unexpectedly, Isaiah was given a glimpse of the greatness and holiness of God. He saw God, first of all, as a glorious, sovereign King sitting on the throne, 'high and exalted' (Isa. 6:1). It was a breathtaking scene. His sight of the majesty of God was heightened when Isaiah saw that 'The train of his robe filled the temple.' The 'train' is a reference to the long, flowing robes a king wore when he sat on the throne to discuss officially the affairs of state. No one was able to stand near because the robes filled the entire temple. Here is a reminder for us that God is awesome and unapproachable.

Not surprisingly, Isaiah was silenced. All he could do was to gaze in wonder and fear on such a great God. Encircling the divine throne were the seraphim, or angels, whom Isaiah saw worshipping and serving God. Each seraph covered its face with two wings because the sight of God overwhelmed even these pure, angelic creatures. With two more wings, they covered their feet as an expression of humility and submission. In unison, they shouted the praises of God, saying,

> Holy, holy, holy is the Lord Almighty;
> the whole earth is full of his glory

> (Isa. 6:3).

Their praises caused the door posts and foundations of the temple to shake, while smoke, symbolizing the presence of God, filled the place. It was an unforgettable sight.

The sinner is condemned

Gripped by this sight of the holy God, Isaiah felt both guilty and condemned. 'Woe to me!' he shouted out (Isa. 6:5). It was an agonizing cry. The word 'woe' indicates his fear that something dreadful was about to happen and crush him. 'I am ruined!' he exclaimed, as he saw himself guilty before God and doomed to die.

Why did he feel condemned? He provides the reasons for us: 'For I am a man of unclean lips.' This was the first reason, and it expresses his complete unworthiness to praise God. His words had often been sinful; this was also true of the people among whom he lived. The second reason is explanatory and foundational; he says, 'My eyes have seen the King, the Lord Almighty.' This is the key, namely, an awareness of the greatness and holiness of God.

Similarly, if you see the greatness of God, you can never be the same again. Compared with the holy God, you begin to see yourself as being dirty and sinful. There is nothing to be proud of in your life. In fact, like Isaiah, you feel guilty and condemned before such a God.

Perhaps you have not yet seen God as one who is great and holy. You need, therefore, to understand what the angels meant when Isaiah heard them praising God and declaring, 'Holy, holy, holy is the Lord Almighty.' Pause, then, for a moment to consider God's holy character. There are three basic facts concerning God's holiness which you need to grasp.

God is holy

First of all, God is holy in his nature. Holiness is not something which God decides to be or something he puts on for a period of time and then pulls off again. For example, I am writing this while sitting at my desk on a warm Saturday morning early in June. Earlier this morning, I walked to the nearby woods with our family dog. It was cool as we set out so I decided to wear a pullover. And I was glad of the extra warmth especially when we were walking in the shade and cool of the trees for several minutes. However, before reaching home again, we spent some time walking in the warmth of the sun and our twelve-year-old dog, a cross between a Labrador and a collie, began to look decidedly hot and tired. Once indoors, she stretched out on the carpet and I took off my pullover. Now, as I write, I am wearing a thin, short-sleeved summer shirt. The point I am making is simple but basic. For God, holiness is not an item like a pullover, or even an attitude or mood, which he can put on and pull off at random as he pleases. That is impossible because holiness belongs to the very nature and essence of God. As such, holiness is inseparable from God; he cannot stop being holy because this is what God is essentially like.

This means that God does not have to decide to be holy. You may decide to improve and change your life. And perhaps the decision is long overdue. Bad habits, lies, selfish behaviour and cruel words have made you feel ashamed. Now you want to live differently. By contrast, God never has to decide to be different or better, for he is always holy. That is his nature and it is impossible for him to be otherwise. Even at Calvary, God did not stop being holy, for there he punished his own beloved Son, the Lord Jesus, as a substitute for our sin. Because his nature is holy, his attitude to sin does not change. 'There is no one holy like the Lord' (1 Sam. 2:2).

God is perfect

Secondly, holiness means that God is free of all sin. It is not easy for us to appreciate this point. After all, we are surrounded by people who sin, and we ourselves sin too. Certainly sin stares us in the face all the time. Hatred, murder, theft, rape, abuse, lying and immorality are only a few of the sins we hear about or witness daily in one way or another. We have never met a perfect human being. Even those people we respect and admire are far from being perfect and sinless. By contrast, however, God never sins and cannot sin. There is no trace of evil or imperfection in his nature. 'God is light; in him there is no darkness at all' (1 John 1:5). But there is even more for us to understand about God's holiness.

God hates sin

Thirdly, because God is holy he hates sin with an intense hatred. Any deviation on our part from his law, which mirrors his pure nature, is hateful to God. It is not merely that God does not like us to sin. Nor is it just a matter that God tolerates sin. There is much more involved. Quite literally, God cannot stand sin. All sin, whatever it may be, is offensive to God:

> You are not a God who takes pleasure in evil;
>   with you the wicked cannot dwell...
>   you hate all who do wrong
>
> (Ps. 5:4-5).

We hate some forms of sin ourselves. The physical abuse of a child, the rape of a young woman, the violent attack on a defenceless old-age pensioner, or the barbaric treatment of adults and children in the cause of 'ethnic cleansing' in the former Yugoslavia all provoke strong responses of anger and hatred from us. But such hatred on our part has to be multiplied millions and millions of times before it can approximate to God's hatred of all sin. And it is because God hates sin that he punishes sinners.

God is angry

It is necessary now to refer to God's anger. However, we need to remove any possible misunderstanding from the outset. To speak of God being angry does not mean he is irritable, bad-tempered, or unpredictable in his reactions. That is not true at all. In fact, anger, or wrath, is an essential quality belonging to the character of God. As such, anger describes the controlled and permanent opposition of God's holy nature to all sin. Such opposition to sin on God's part is not a whim, or a mere decision or occasional mood, but the reaction of his perfect holy nature to sin. Anger, then, is as essential to the nature of God as is love; without anger God would cease to be God.

It may surprise you to know that there are more references in the Bible to the anger and wrath of God than there are to the love of God. There are in the Old Testament alone, for example, over twenty Hebrew words used to describe the wrath of God and these words are used nearly 600 times. The New Testament retains and develops even more fully this emphasis on divine wrath.

We can now gather together some of the threads from chapters 19 and 20. Sin in our lives does matter. It often matters to, and affects, other people, but our sin *always* matters to God. He hates sin and is angry towards sinners. And we are all, without a single exception, guilty.

We are in danger

This puts us in an extremely dangerous situation. God is angry with us and threatens to punish us for our sin. It is no idle threat, either. The Bible makes it clear that this anger is not something God keeps to himself and hides from people. Rather it is an anger God is continually revealing towards sinners. 'The wrath of God', declares the Bible, 'is being revealed from heaven against all the godlessness and wickedness of men' (Rom. 1:18). The tense of the verb in Greek means such anger 'is continually being revealed'.

Consider God's anger as it was expressed a long time ago in the days of Noah. Only Noah and his small family trusted and obeyed the Lord. Part of Noah's work was to preach repentance, but the people were not interested at all in God. They imagined they were having a good time. All they were really interested in was eating, drinking and getting married. Patiently God waited. He waited for over a hundred years. Eventually God ordered Noah to take his family into the ark and then he flooded the world in his anger and destroyed the rest of the human race (read Genesis chapters 6-9). His threats were not idle threats at all. God really is angry against sin.

Some time later God was angry with the cities of Sodom and Gomorrah because the people sinned greatly and practised some of the most base sexual sins, including homosexuality (Genesis chapters 18-19). God destroyed these cities by fire.

Not even Israel, God's chosen people, escaped the anger of God. Whether in the wilderness, or in the period of the judges, or during the monarchy, or prior to the exile in Babylon, God's anger was regularly expressed against their sin and unbelief. The destruction of both the temple and the city of Jerusalem in 586 B.C. and again, but more devastatingly, in A.D. 70, were expressions of God's wrath on the nation of Israel.

Many more examples could be given but the fact you must reckon with is this: the holy God is angry towards sinners. Although there is danger ahead, many people do not realize their predicament, nor do they heed the warning signs. What this danger facing sinners is will be spelt out in the next chapter.

22.
Danger

Danger — we all face it in one way or another, although some are at greater risk than others. There can be danger even in a family situation. Annual statistics disclose that in the small country of Wales where I live, in one year 1,302 women and 2,112 children were given shelter in refuges run by Women's Aid groups. These women and children had fled their homes because of domestic violence. In some areas, there is danger living on a housing estate. The residents of one housing estate I know of sometimes give the nickname 'Alcatraz' to the estate in recognition of the fact that life can be hard and dangerous there. Almost daily in the national news there are reports of people (often elderly) being viciously attacked and sometimes murdered in their own homes.

Danger lurks in places of employment, too, and sometimes there are tragic accidents. I am reminded of the dangers faced by coalminers, many of whom have been injured or killed while working at the coalface.

Politicians also face dangers: some are abused, others are physically attacked and a few are murdered by opponents or fanatics. The names of John F. Kennedy and Martin Luther King come immediately to mind. Mikhail Gorbachev faced danger when he was President of the former Soviet Republic.

We should not deceive ourselves, however. Danger faces all of us, albeit in different ways. Even sunbathing exposes us to the harmful UV-B and UV-A rays. Ultraviolet B is known to cause cancer, while Ultraviolet A penetrates deep below the skin. With the depletion of the ozone layer and people taking longer and sunnier holidays, the incidence of skin cancers has rocketed in places as far apart as the United Kingdom and Australia. Reports of new cancer cases in the United Kingdom increased significantly in the months after the Chernobyl power station disaster in Ukraine. One major contributory factor was probably radioactive fall-out in rainfall. There is corroboratory evidence from Ukraine, where the number of children under fifteen suffering from thyroid cancer has shown an increase of nearly 8,000 per cent. The danger is real.

Children who live with an adult smoker inhale the nicotine equivalent of up to 150 cigarettes every year. Statistics show that the children of smokers visit the doctor more often, take more prescriptions and are admitted to hospital more times than children in non-smoking households. Parental smoking is reckoned to leave children twice as likely to suffer asthma symptoms and respiratory infections.

Or who would have thought of the danger lurking for young backpackers in the Belanglo State Forest in Australia? Deep inside the forest, a ruthless serial killer stabbed more than seven young people to death over a period of three years and concealed their bodies under a thin blanket of leaves and bracken. Each victim went missing on the Hume Highway, south of Sydney, during daylight hours and also on a public holiday. The New South Wales Police spokesman declared, 'This is one of the most horrific series of crimes we have ever come across, and we are determined to search every inch of that forest.' In the meantime, backpackers and others were warned of the danger and urged to take the necessary precautions.

The danger of hell

There is another danger, however, that I want to refer to, one people are often unaware of. Let me explain. Our sins matter to God; he is not indifferent to our sins, nor is he able to ignore them. The reason for this, as we have already seen, is that God's nature is holy. By God's anger, or wrath, the Bible refers to the way in which this holy God reacts necessarily against all sin by punishing the guilty persons. The climax of this punishment for unbelievers is at death when they are assigned by God to hell. Hell is an awful place and infinitely more dreadful then a Hiroshima or a nuclear war. Let us pause for a moment to ponder why it is such a dreadful place.

Separation

The Lord Jesus described hell in terms of separation. Concluding his famous Sermon on the Mount in Matthew's Gospel, chapter 7, the Lord describes unbelievers at the last day pleading to enter heaven. These unbelievers had seen the power of God at work in other people's lives but, tragically, they themselves had never been converted. They were only religious, and were strangers to the transforming work of the Holy Spirit in their lives. It is to these people that the Lord Jesus says, 'I never knew you. Away from me' (Matt. 7:23).

On another occasion, the Lord describes himself judging all the peoples of the world at the final judgement. Once again he tells unbelievers, 'Depart from me, you who are cursed, into the eternal fire prepared for the devil and his angels' (Matt. 25:41). Ponder the significance of the word 'depart' which the Lord uses. To be told to 'depart' means that you are rejected by Christ the Judge. He refuses to allow you into heaven. The door is shut firmly in your face. In this way, you are removed from his mercy and help. There is no hope for you ever again. If this happens to you, your plight will be a terrible one indeed.

Punishment

Separation from Christ, the only one who is able to rescue you, will be dreadful; however, it is only one aspect of hell's sufferings for unbelievers. Another feature of hell is punishment. Yes, God actually punishes sinners in hell and he is perfectly fair in doing so. 'They will go away to eternal punishment,' declares Jesus Christ, 'but the righteous to eternal life' (Matt. 25:46). And the word used here really means punishment.

But how does God punish sinners in hell? Our Lord teaches that the body as well as the soul of the unbeliever will be punished eventually in hell. This is what he says: 'Do not be afraid of those who kill the body but cannot kill the soul. Rather, be afraid of the One who can destroy both soul and body in hell' (Matt. 10:28).

Conscience, too, will inflict misery on unbelievers in hell. 'It is better for you to enter into life maimed than with two hands to go into hell,' our Lord warns, '... where their worm does not die, and the fire is not quenched' (Mark 9:43-48). A 'nagging' conscience can be a major problem in our lives here on earth; our consciences accuse and condemn us for things we have done. For some, the condemning voice of conscience can be so loud and incessant that they have to turn to drink or drugs or even suicide in order to quieten it. In hell, however, conscience will whip and condemn unbelievers more fiercely than ever before. There will be no peace of mind for them and no mercy. The Lord describes one rich unbeliever as being in hell and 'in torment' (Luke 16:23; cf. Rev. 20:10). Such torments and pangs of conscience find expression in great anguish, despair, weeping and gnashing of teeth, all of which highlight the punitive aspect of hell's sufferings for unbelievers (cf. Matt. 8:12; 13:50; Mark 9:43-48; Luke 16:23-28; Rev.14:10; 21:8).

Symbolism

But is there a literal 'hell fire'? Descriptions like 'eternal fire' (Matt. 18:8; Jude 7), and 'in this fire' (Luke 16:24) refer to hell. What do these descriptions mean? Clearly symbolism is being used to underline and illustrate the fact of punishment. The symbolism points to something which is indescribably terrible — so terrible, in fact, that it is essential to use this kind of picture-language to describe it. What, then, does the symbolism of fire point to?

Two Bible verses help to answer the question for us. The first is in Deuteronomy 4:24: 'For the Lord your God is a consuming fire, a jealous God.' A similar statement appears in Hebrews 12:29: 'For our God is a consuming fire.' These two statements refer to the fire of God's anger towards sin. God it is who makes hell so terrible for unbelievers. His anger is like a fierce, never-ending fire, justly punishing unbelievers in hell without ever destroying them. Both in the realm of the body and of the soul unbelievers will suffer the fire of God's wrath without being themselves consumed, just as in a very different situation the three Hebrews in Babylon stood inside the burning furnace without being burnt in any way (Daniel chapter 3).

To answer our question, the 'fire' of hell represents the fierce anger of God upon sinners continually in hell. It really 'is a dreadful thing to fall into the hands of the living God' (Heb. 10:31). And, what is even more sad, there will be no end to this punishment. There is no possibility of their escaping from hell or having any ease in their sufferings there. Hell is for ever and ever. And that is not my opinion but the teaching of the Lord Jesus Christ, who says, 'Depart from me, you who are cursed, into the eternal fire,' and, later, says of the same people, 'They will go away to eternal punishment' (Matt. 25:41,46). On another occasion, the Lord urged people to resist sin even if this involved drastic action because, 'It is better for you to enter life maimed or crippled than to have two hands or two feet and be thrown into eternal fire' (Matt. 18:8-9). Just as God and heaven are eternal, so hell will also be eternal.

A substitute

But there is good news! The holy God who has been offended and sinned against has taken the initiative in providing a substitute to suffer the sinner's punishment: '... whom God has set forth to be a propitiation through faith in his blood' (Rom. 3:25, AV). When the sins of the elect were laid upon Jesus Christ on the cross, the wrath of God was unleashed upon him. The punishment they deserve to suffer was willingly taken by the Lord Jesus. Without question, Calvary is the greatest and most wonderful rescue operation in the world's history. In the next chapters we will find out more about what Jesus Christ achieved on the cross.

Section IV
The cross: God's answer

23.
The cross

I have now visited Korea several times but each time I have been impressed by the warmth and kindness of the people as well as the beauty of their mountainous country. As I travelled extensively within the country by train and coach on my first visit in 1991, I was moved as I saw that all the Protestant churches, whether in the countryside, towns or cities, displayed a large, illuminated cross in a prominent position on their buildings. As the train sped through a town or village I could see crosses lit up in different colours on church buildings over a wide radius. It was a reminder, of course, that the death of Jesus Christ is important; the cross is a sign of our salvation and it should be the glory of churches.

There are many kinds of crosses, too: gold, jewelled, wooden, stone, iron and even plastic crosses. Some of these crosses are distinctive, such as Celtic, Crusaders' or Coptic crosses. Then there is the bare cross, the crucifix and the *Christus Rex*; the latter depicts Christ crowned and in royal attire on the cross. You will find huge crosses in the Andes and in the Alps, as well as small crosses on the dashboards of cars or taxis and on gravestones. The cross is a familiar symbol.

Some time ago my attention was drawn to an unusual photograph in a daily newspaper. The caption above the photograph was: 'Ex-Disciple has a cross to bear.' In the photograph, Kevin 'Mad-dog' Mudford was riding his motor-cycle and, at the same time, pulling a huge wooden cross. While the weight of the cross rested on his right shoulder, a wheel had been attached to the base of the cross so that it could be pulled easily. What was the point of pulling such a big cross on his motorcycle? Mudford had been the leader of a gang in Australia called the 'Devil's Disciples' and at the early age of fifteen was charged with murder. In his thirties, however, there was a dramatic change in his life. After hearing the Christian gospel and that the Lord Jesus had died for sinners in bearing their punishment, Mudford trusted personally in Jesus Christ. Immediately he had peace with God and enjoyed the forgive-ness of his sins through the sacrifice of the Lord Jesus on the cross. His life was transformed and the work of the Lord on the cross became very special and important to him. He now spends his time travelling around Australia teaching the Chris-tian gospel and also pulling a huge cross.

Re-enactments of the crucifixion

Sometimes churches try to re-enact at Easter time the crucifix-ion of Jesus Christ in order to make the cross more meaningful and real to local people and visitors. The streets may be brought to a standstill as hundreds of people arrive in one town to attend the Easter Pageant portraying the last days of the life of Jesus Christ. A final scene is a large cross placed in the town centre; a local man usually plays the part of Jesus but he is strapped rather than nailed to the cross. 'The aim of the performance is to remind people what Easter is about,' the organizers claim. 'A lot of people forget the real reason why we celebrate Easter.' And that, sadly, is a fact.

In some countries, the re-enactment of the crucifixion is even more realistic. I have in front of me newspaper photographs taken in April 1990 in the Philippines of individuals being crucified. More than twenty Filipino worshippers were nailed to crosses as the predominantly 'Christian' nation marked Good Friday. One woman took part in her fourteenth Good Friday 'crucifixion'. Another participant, a forty-year-old taxi driver, said that he pledged to undergo the ten-minute ritual at Kapitangan in the Philippines to give thanks for the recovery of his mother from a serious illness. One horrific photograph shows a Filipino dressed as a Roman guard, hammering a nail into the palm of Chito Sangelang, re-enacting the nailing of Christ to the cross.

At the same time in another country, thousands of people thronged the Via Dolorosa in Jerusalem's Old City to walk in the footsteps of Jesus to what is traditionally regarded as the site of his crucifixion in the heart of the walled Old City's Christian quarter. An American pilgrim, dressed as Jesus in blood-stained robes and dragging a giant cross, was whipped by two other men dressed as Roman soldiers, while a woman, dressed as his mother, pleaded for him.

In the West, one of the better known re-enactments of the Lord's passion takes place every ten years in the village of Oberammergau in Bavaria, just fifty miles away from Munich. It originated from the plague which gripped Bavaria in 1633, when the villagers promised that if they survived they would stage a production every ten years about Christ's crucifixion. They have kept their promise, too. Lasting for five hours, it vividly brings the words of the Bible to life through acted scenes, tableaux and a sung commentary. About 2,000 of the 5,000 villagers participate, including a forty-eight-strong choir and an orchestra. The crucifixion scene enacted there has a note of reality about it. Three large crosses are erected with a man on each cross, representing the two thieves and Jesus Christ. But nails are not hammered into the men's hands or feet; they are held securely to the crosses by means of a

foothold and hand grips. Around the three crosses, villagers
are dressed up as priests, soldiers and spectators.

The centrality of the cross to the Christian faith

Whatever your views may be about re-enacting the crucifixion
or using the symbol of the cross in various ways, one fact is
undeniable: the cross is the central symbol of Christianity. We
can go further, too. The cross is central to the Christian faith;
indeed, without the cross, there is no Christian gospel and no
salvation. What is important, then, is not the image, or symbol,
or re-enactment of the cross, but the work which Jesus Christ
did there. His work on the cross was unique and crucial for us.
Everything depends on what he did on that cross. Did he really
rescue us? Has he reconciled sinners to God? Was his work on
the cross final and adequate in dealing with our sin problem?
'Yes, and yes again' is the authoritative, reassuring answer
provided by the Bible, the Word of God. Listen to the way in
which the point is underlined: 'He has reconciled you by
Christ's physical body through death to present you holy in his
[God's] sight, without blemish and free from accusation' (Col.
1:22). What Jesus Christ did on the cross was successful. And
it is glorious news. Not only are we reconciled to the holy God,
but the sins of believers no longer condemn them because the
Lord Jesus Christ died on their behalf.

This fact is repeated again and again. In Revelation, for
example, we are told that Jesus Christ 'has freed us from our
sins by his blood' (Rev. 1:5) and, later, this truth is the subject
of praise: 'With your blood you purchased men for God' (Rev.
5:9). Similarly, Paul tells us, 'He forgave us all our sins, having
cancelled the written code, with its regulations, that was
against us and that stood opposed to us; he took it away, nailing
it to the cross' (Col. 2:13-14). Freedom, a purchase-price,

forgiveness and the removal of legitimate accusations were all obtained on the cross by the Lord Jesus. His work on the cross was not only completed; it was also successful and fruitful. Christians owe everything to what he did there on the cross.

A challenge

Here is a challenge for you. Turn your thoughts away from the mere symbol of the cross. Instead, focus your attention on the one who suffered and died there. But do not stop even there. Consider in detail the work this glorious person achieved there. To help you, in the following chapters we will look at some of the key terms and categories used in the New Testament to describe the work of Jesus Christ in rescuing us.

24.
Sacrifice

The message is loud and clear, namely, that the death of Jesus Christ on the cross was a sacrifice — to God. This is the emphasis and teaching of the Bible. For example, we are told that 'Christ loved us and gave himself up for us as a fragrant offering and sacrifice to God' (Eph. 5:2). Another statement reveals that Christ 'has appeared once for all at the end of the ages to do away with sin by the sacrifice of himself' (Heb. 9:26). Not only does the word 'sacrifice' appear in these two statements, but it is important to notice that the work of Jesus Christ on the cross is conceived *primarily* in terms of sacrifice. There are also numerous indirect references in the New Testament which assume that the Lord's death was sacrificial. This was true of John the Baptist when, pointing to Jesus Christ, he excitedly announced, 'Look, the Lamb of God, who takes away the sin of the world!' (John 1:29). Similarly, the apostle John was granted a vision of the Lord Jesus in heaven and heard the heavenly choir singing his praises, 'because you were slain, and with your blood you purchased men for God' (Rev. 5:9). The language is one of sacrifice.

Today we use the word 'sacrifice' frequently and in many different ways. My parents sacrificed in order to help me enter higher education. It was difficult for them because they were poor, working-class parents already struggling to make ends meet. Nevertheless, they denied themselves luxuries and even necessities in order to assist me. It was a sacrifice, yet one prompted by love. For someone else, it may be the decision to give up a good job or refuse a marriage proposal in order to care for sick parents. And the sacrifice involved is considerable. Or think of athletes who sacrifice personal enjoyments for a strict diet and demanding routines of training in order to compete in their chosen sport. We also speak of soldiers who in times of war sacrifice their lives in order to defend their country and achieve freedom. In order to rescue a person at sea, or in deep underground caves, or a coalmine, or on a mountain, the rescue services are exposed to considerable danger. Not infrequently, a member of the rescue team may himself be killed in the rescue operation. His courage and endeavours are praised while his own death is sometimes spoken of in terms of a sacrifice. We know what is meant. The person concerned disregarded the risks to his own life in a valiant attempt to help someone in danger. Examples can be multiplied but in one way or another the elements of danger, cost, self-denial and effort are involved in the sacrifices people make for one another.

The background to the sacrifice of Christ

In order to understand the sacrifice of the Lord Jesus on the cross, it is necessary to refer once again to the Old Testament background and the different sacrifices which were offered in the temple. There were four main categories of offerings in the Old Testament: the burnt offering, the peace or 'fellowship' offering, the sin offering and the guilt offering. While the majority of offerings were sacrifices, there were a few which did not require the killing of an animal or bird. One example was the cereal or grain offering, which was comprised mainly of fine flour, unleavened bread, wafers and either cakes or ears of grain. Part of this offering was burned with incense following the burnt or peace offerings. There were special occasions which demanded this cereal offering, as in the ritual cleansing of a leper (Lev. 14:10,20-31) and the fulfilment of a Nazarite vow (Num. 6:15-21). What is important to notice, however, is that the most important offerings involved the sacrificing of animals; such sacrifices were necessary before people could approach and worship God. Their sin was covered in this way and they were then free to dedicate themselves as well as to share fellowship together.

The subject of animal sacrifices in the Old Testament has already been explored in detail in chapter 3, where we tried to understand the purpose of sacrificing animals and the need for it. The importance of the term 'blood' in the Bible now needs to be re-emphasized. Blood was proof that the death of the victim had occurred. In the case of the animal sacrifices in the Old Testament, the animal was killed and its blood was later sprinkled on the altar as evidence that it was dead. This was necessary because God's anger needs to be turned away from the sinner. Because of his holy nature, which makes him hate sin, God must punish sin. However, the divine anger towards us is averted only when the substitute is punished and killed in our place, and this is what Jesus Christ did on the cross. The Old Testament animal sacrifices pointed forward to this one unique and final sacrifice of the Lord Jesus Christ at Calvary.

An example will help us to see this relationship more clearly. As humans who are also sinful it is impossible for us to enter God's presence just as we are. That truth is underlined in the sacrificial system of the Old Testament and especially on the Day of Atonement. Let me remind you of the occasion and background.

The Day of Atonement

One day the Lord directed Moses to warn his brother Aaron not to enter the inner sanctuary of the temple whenever he pleased, '... or else he will die' (Lev. 16:2). Although he was the high priest, Aaron was not entitled to enter God's presence. The inner sanctuary, also called the 'Most Holy Place' and the 'Holy of Holies', symbolized the presence of the holy, awesome God; there the ark of the covenant, containing the law, was also located. To enter that sacred room without divine permission and preparation would involve instant death. God must be approached on his own terms.

On one special day each year, however, God permitted the high priest to enter the inner sanctuary, but there were conditions which had to be observed. Only one man, that is, the high priest, could enter and that just once a year, and even this high-ranking official had to observe various rituals. For example, he had to have a bath and then wear plain white clothes, symbolizing his moral purity. Sacrifices were offered for himself and his family and the high priest sprinkled the victim's blood on the lid of the ark in the inner sanctuary. Then he took two male goats and a ram as offerings to God on behalf of the nation (Lev. 16:3,5). One goat was chosen as a sacrifice to God for the sins of the people; when it had been killed, its blood was taken into the inner sanctuary and sprinkled on top of the ark, 'because of the uncleanness and rebellion of the Israelites, whatever their sins have been' (Lev. 16:16). The other goat was sent away into the wilderness, symbolically carrying all the people's sins away. Sin had been dealt with, at least ceremonially, and in a way which pointed to, and found fulfilment in, Christ's work on the cross.

This Day of Atonement is probably part of the background to statements in 2 Corinthians 5:21 and Galatians 3:13 concerning Christ's work on the cross. However, it is in the letter

to the Hebrews where it receives more detailed attention. Two
points are emphasized there with regard to what the Lord Jesus
achieved on the cross.

The way opened into God's presence

First of all, by his sacrifice he opened the door for his people
to enter God's holy presence regularly, not just once a year as
in the case of the high priest. The barriers preventing access to
God have been removed. Ponder the exciting news. The Lord
Jesus 'entered the Most Holy Place once for all by his own
blood, having obtained eternal redemption' (Heb. 9:12). For
believers, it means, 'We have confidence to enter the Most Holy
Place by the blood of Jesus, by a new and living way opened
for us through the curtain, that is, his body' (Heb. 10:19-21).
What glorious news! I am no longer barred from God's holy
presence because of my sins. Nor is God going to punish me
for my sin if I approach him. And this is due entirely to the
sacrifice of the Lord Jesus. On the cross, he suffered the punishment due to us because of our sins and satisfied the just law
of God in our place.

Forgiveness

Secondly, by his sacrifice the Lord has won forgiveness for us.
Both the sacrifices, as well as the sending of a goat into the
desert area, pointed to the forgiveness of sin. It is impossible
for the blood of animals to obtain forgiveness (Heb. 10:4);
these animal sacrifices only pointed to the one final and unique
sacrifice of Jesus Christ on the cross. He it is who obtains
forgiveness for us.

   In December 1992, the young widow of a murdered police
sergeant in England explained why she could not forgive her

husband's killer. Her voice tense with emotion, she explained that she blamed the killer, not only for her husband's death, but also for the subsequent death of her elderly parents who were devastated by the murder. 'I can never forgive him,' she emphasized, 'for what has happened.' Her feelings are understandable. Certainly her loss was enormous and irreparable. You would expect God to speak to us like that. After all, our sins against God can be counted in their millions. And, remember, because God is holy, he hates and punishes sin. It seems as if God could never forgive us. But wait a moment! God has found a way to forgive us, and a way which is both just and glorious.

Another illustration may help us at this point. About four years ago, Brian and Ursula Randall paid the 'supreme sacrifice' trying to save their daughter from a knife-man. Sarah, the twenty-year-old daughter, survived thirty-seven stab wounds but she was shielded from otherwise inevitable death by her parents. They were courageous and unselfish; their concern was the safety of their daughter but in the process they were themselves murdered. Their action points to the far more wonderful love and sacrifice of Jesus Christ who, on the cross, rescued and shielded us from the punishment of our own sins: 'Christ loved us and gave himself up for us as a fragrant offering and sacrifice to God' (Eph. 5:2). It was a costly sacrifice but one the Lord Jesus was willing to make in our place. His sacrifice was acceptable to God the Father for he himself was perfect, yet, as our substitute, he bore on the cross the divine wrath against sin, a wrath which we deserved as sinners. Because of this unique sacrifice, God now offers free and full forgiveness to all who believe on the Lord Jesus. Christ's sacrifice on Calvary was final, perfect and sufficient; we need no other. As believers, we offer praise, good works, generous gifts (Heb. 13:15-16; Phil. 4:18) and our bodies (Rom. 12:1) as thank offerings and spiritual sacrifices to God in response to his great love.

25.
Redemption:
freed — but at a price

The meaning in the Bible of words like 'redeem' and 'redemption' is clear. No doubt you have already guessed it from the title of this chapter. Yes, redemption means freedom, but on payment of a price. On the cross, the Lord Jesus paid the price to set people free from the slavery of their sin and, at the same time, to make them God's willing people and servants. Redemption spells deliverance. That is exactly what Christ achieved for sinners by his unique sacrifice.

Freedom is a glorious reality in all kinds of ways. A patient, for example, is discharged by the medical doctors and is free to leave hospital and go home. It is a marvellous feeling. Or it may be a teenager who obtains the necessary examination grades and, as a result, is free to embark on a university course. Perhaps you have obtained a visa granting you freedom to enter a certain country. You wish to visit this country and now you are free to go because of the visa. Sometimes an animal is trapped in a hole or cave and is eventually freed by rescuers, to the delight of its owners.

For Nelson Mandela, his arrest in 1962 led to a prison sentence for life. With six others, he was taken to the stone cells of Robben Island, off Cape Town, where he was forced to break rocks for more than twelve years until his transfer to a mainland jail. He refused to bargain for his release and rejected offers of liberty in exile. On Robben Island, in Cape Town's modern Pollsmoor Prison and then alone in a prison bungalow among the vineyards of Paarl, he served his long prison sentence. For twenty-five years he was allowed no more than two forty-minute visits a month from his family. The campaign for his release reached a climax on Mandela's seventieth birthday on 18 July 1988, a month before he was transferred to hospital with tuberculosis. He was eventually released in 1990 and thousands of his followers celebrated by shouting and displaying messages like, 'He's free.'

Or think of hostage-negotiator Terry Waite, who was held captive in an underground cell in Beirut for 1,763 days, usually blindfolded and half-naked. There were endless periods of solitary confinement. Chained to the wall, he was unable to stand or even to lie straight. Then there were times when they roused him from sleep to beat him: 'They would wake me in the middle of the night,' Waite remarked, 'and beat me with cable on the soles of my feet, which is very painful.' He was even threatened with execution on one occasion and told, 'You have five hours to live.' Eventually, he was freed and returned, thankfully, to England.

November 1989 was significant for the the people of East Berlin as they celebrated their new-found freedom. It was in 1961 that the Communist government had built the Berlin wall to stop the flow of their citizens to the West. One of the first things the people did in November 1989 was to start breaking the famous wall down with their hammers, chisels and even machinery as an expression of their new liberty and the reunification of the German nation. They were free again!

The Passover

Redemption is one of several words and concepts used in the Bible to describe freedom and deliverance. Another important concept is that of the Passover. When the Israelites were in harsh slavery in Egypt, God sent his servant Moses to lead his people out to freedom. Pharaoh, the Egyptian leader, resisted the plan with all his might. However, this was the platform for the display of God's power in which he inflicted nine different plagues on the Egyptians. The last one involved the death of all the first-born males of Egypt. It was a disaster for them. By contrast, the Israelites were spared, but only by placing some of the blood of the sacrificial lamb or kid around their doorframes (Exod. 12:7). The sprinkling of the blood on the door was essential. 'The blood will be a sign for you on the houses where you are,' the Lord declared, 'and when I see the blood, I will pass over you. No destructive plague will touch you when I strike Egypt' (Exod. 12:13). That is exactly what happened. The Egyptians had suffered enough and the Israelites were allowed by Pharaoh to leave the country and slavery. Quickly, they left almost immediately after this Passover meal and began the long march to their promised land.

One of the commands given them by God was that they should observe the Passover feast annually in remembrance of God's deliverance (Exod. 12:14-15). Before his own sacrifice, the Lord Jesus observed the Passover meal with his disciples. His death on the cross happened during the Passover time. 'Christ, our Passover lamb,' declares the apostle Paul, 'has been sacrificed' (1 Cor. 5:7). He freed us on the cross; that is, he frees us as Christians from the slavery of sin and from all evil powers. In the context of 1 Corinthians 5:7, it means we should make a complete break with all sin in our lives.

Redemption — the background

Redemption, like the Passover, also denotes deliverance and this is the concept which will be developed now to describe an aspect of Christ's work on the cross. You may not be familiar with the related words 'redemption' or 'redeem'. However, when used by the Lord Jesus and the apostles, these words were familiar to everyone, whether from a Gentile or Jewish background. They were everyday words which people understood and used. But freedom was only a part of the meaning, for 'redemption' and 'redeem' go further by telling us specifically how this freedom was obtained. It was freedom on payment of a price.

We shall pause briefly to consider the background, in order to appreciate the significance of 'redemption' in describing the cross. In Greek culture, there were many examples of redemption. For instance, when the Greek armies were victorious in battle it was customary for them to make slaves of the defeated soldiers. And if a slave was an important person at home then money was often raised from among his people and sent to buy him back. In this way the person was 'redeemed' and the one responsible for the transaction was a 'redeemer', while the payment made for the release was known as the 'ransom'. The whole process was known as 'redemption'.

A similar process and language were involved in freeing ordinary slaves. Even a slave could struggle to save money in order to buy his freedom. It could take him a long time, however, to save the ransom price and it was a difficult process negotiating freedom as well as observing the different customs and rituals of their pagan religions.

One fact here intrigues me. Usually, the word used by the Greeks for the act of redemption was *'lytrosis'*. Whenever the New Testament writers use the word, however (and it is used altogether ten times), they always use a longer form with the prefix, *'apo'*. This compound form of the word, used in the New Testament, was unusual in Greek literature and serves to underline the unique redemption purchased by the Lord Jesus Christ.

For the Jews, the term 'redemption' was exceptionally rich in significance. One important aspect was that of a kinsman who took over the responsibilities of caring for a family when a man died without children. Boaz, for example, acted as a kinsman-redeemer when he cared for the widow Ruth and eventually married her (Ruth 4:1-12). There were other situations, too, in which redemption was necessary. If a poor man sold himself into slavery in order to clear his debts, it was possible to redeem him (Lev. 25:47-48). Nevertheless, redemption was obtained only by the slave's relatives paying the ransom price. Similar rules applied for the redemption of property, such as a house or field.

In the Old Testament, God is described as redeeming his people (eg. Exod. 6:6; Ps. 77:14-15; Prov. 23:10-11; Isa 43:3-4; Jer. 50:33-34), but these references all highlight the fact of God's power being exercised in favour of his people. He did not pay a ransom price to anyone. Such a suggestion would be absurd with regard to God himself. Nevertheless, his rescue of Israel involved the exercise of divine power, referred to as God's 'outstretched arm' (Exod. 6:6) or 'right hand' (Exod. 15:12). Even here there is a hint of the redemption concept. In other words, the divine redemption of Israel was costly to God. It was not without effort or cost. For God, redemption involved the exertion of great power.

Christ's redemption

Against this background, we are now in a position to appreciate the significance of Christ's redemption on the cross. Remember, we all need to be freed from the power of sin in our lives. Sin is a cruel master and tyrant, enslaving human beings worldwide. The point is taught clearly by the Lord Jesus himself. 'If you hold to my teaching,' he declared, 'you are really my disciples. Then you will know the truth, and the truth will set you free' (John 8:31-32). The Jews took exception to the statement and its implications. They were indignant. After all, they had never been slaves to anyone, so they thought. Why, then, talk about freedom? The Lord's reply was emphatic and uncompromising: 'I tell you the truth, everyone who sins is a slave to sin' (John 8:33-34). And it is a fact; sin is a strong, active force within our lives. We need to be freed from its grip, and this is something we cannot do ourselves.

But this is exactly what the Lord Jesus came to do on our behalf. 'For even the Son of Man', he explained, 'did not come to be served, but to serve, and to give his life as a ransom for many' (Mark 10:45). Notice the word 'ransom' here. He did not come only to teach, or heal, or provide an example of a perfect life. His prime purpose was 'to give his life as a ransom'. The price to be paid to God for our release was his death, a death not forced upon him but willingly offered on our behalf.

Again, 'Christ redeemed us from the curse of the law by becoming a curse for us,' writes the apostle Paul (Gal. 3:13). Here the emphasis is on Christ paying the price for our release by suffering, instead of us, the curse or punishment of the law which we deserve. In the Bible, a curse is usually related to sin (Gen. 3). 'Cursed,' the Lord declares, 'is everyone who does not continue to do everything written in the Book of the Law' (Deut. 27:26). The curse means judgement and punishment because of our sin; this curse of God's broken law rests on us all. Jesus Christ redeemed his people by becoming a curse in their place, that is, the punishment and curse were transferred to him as our substitute.

In Galatians 4:4-5, Christ is said to redeem us from the law itself. The law is viewed here as a method of gaining acceptance with God on the basis of our own human efforts. Redemption is only achieved by Christ's self-sacrifice on the cross. The point is again underlined in Ephesians 1:7: 'In him we have redemption,' but, notice, it is 'through his blood'; that is, the Lord's sacrifice of himself in death on the cross was the payment of a ransom to God which secures our deliverance. He 'obtained eternal redemption', for 'He has died as a ransom to set them free' (Heb. 9:12,15). The ransom price he paid for our release is clearly stated, too: 'It was not with perishable things such as silver and gold that you were redeemed ... but with the precious blood of Christ' (1 Peter 1:18-19).

The redemption of the body

There is also a future, glorious aspect to this redemption Christ obtained for us. Not only are we freed now and enjoy the forgiveness of sins; there is more to come. At the second coming of the Lord Jesus in glory, there will be 'the redemption of our bodies' (Rom. 8:23). If we are alive on earth when Christ returns then our bodies will be changed into the likeness of Christ. For those who have already died, their bodies will be raised and transformed, 'so that they will be like his glorious body' (Phil. 3:21). While we wait as believers for the consummation of redemption, we now have the 'Holy Spirit of God' indwelling us; he it is who has 'sealed' us 'for the day of redemption' (Eph. 4:30). The seal authenticates; it is also a guarantee of more to come. At the end time, when Christ returns, we shall enjoy the fulness of redemption. Christians can look forward to a glorious future, but we owe it all to what Jesus Christ did for us on the cross.

Bought with a price

One more point needs to be made before closing the chapter. In fact, it is made effectively by the apostle Paul in 1 Corinthians 6:19-20: 'You are not your own; you were bought at a price.' Are you a Christian? If so, the Lord Jesus has freed you. He paid the ransom price for your release, both from the power and the punishment of sin. You are free, and it is gloriously true. However, remember that you have also been bought by Christ. He now owns you. His claims over your life are total. 'You are not your own,' declares the apostle Paul.

26.
Propitiation:
God's wrath diverted by sacrifice

'Propitiation' is a big word and one we hardly use today. Nearly all modern translations of the Bible, including the New International Version, avoid using it. Many scholars, too, dislike the word intensely and they radically reinterpret it, as well as substituting for it other words, such as 'expiation'.

One reason why scholars dislike the word is because of their conviction that God is never angry. According to them, therefore, God does not need to be propitiated. Anyway, they insist, the word pictures God as a capricious being who sometimes breaks out in uncontrollable bursts of anger and vindictiveness. But they are wrong. As we saw in chapter 21, God is angry towards sin. This is a fact which the Bible assumes and teaches repeatedly. His anger, however, is not temper, nor is it an outburst of wild rage. Rather, the divine anger is the controlled, necessary reaction of God's holy, sin-hating nature against sin. This is what God is like in his essential nature.

The word 'propitiation', therefore, tells us something extremely important about the sacrifice of Jesus Christ. Quite simply, it means to turn away and divert anger by means of a sacrifice. And that is what the Lord Jesus did when he died for us on the cross. A major diversion took place there. The tidal wave of God's wrath fell on the Lord Jesus. He was made sin for us. 'In my place condemned he stood,' wrote the hymn-writer. Jesus Christ became our substitute. By the sacrifice of himself, the Lord Jesus turned God's anger away from ourselves as sinners; he bore it himself, instead of us. This then is what the word 'propitiation' signifies in the Bible.

The New Testament use of the word

Neither the noun 'propitiation' nor the verb 'propitiate' is used often in the New Testament. The first reference is in Romans 3:25: 'Whom God has set forth to be a propitiation through faith in his blood, to declare his righteousness for the remission of sins that are past' (AV). The NIV translation here is disappointing: 'God presented him as a sacrifice of atonement, through faith in his blood.' In a footnote, however, the NIV translators offer the alternative: 'as the one who would turn aside his wrath'. This alternative translation is a considerable improvement and almost captures the meaning of propitiation.

The same root word is used twice in the first epistle of John: 'And he is the propitiation for our sins: and not for ours only, but also for the sins of the whole world' (1 John 2:2, AV); 'Herein is love, not that we loved God, but that he loved us, and sent his Son to be the propitiation for our sins' (1 John 4:10, AV).

The word is also used in the Greek of Hebrews 9:5, where it is translated in the Authorized Version as 'mercy seat', or in the NIV as 'place of atonement'.

Possibly the best-known reference is Romans 3:25. Dr Martyn Lloyd-Jones described it as 'one of the most important verses in the whole of Scripture ... absolutely crucial for a true understanding of ... [the] way of salvation'.[1] Certainly the verse and the word 'propitiation' take us to the heart of the gospel and tell us clearly what Christ achieved at Calvary.

Propitiation in Christian experience

Many people have in fact been converted to Christ through reading Romans 3:25 or hearing it preached. William Cowper, the hymn-writer, was under conviction of sin in his room one day and in deep agony of soul. He walked around his room many times. There seemed to be no relief for him. His sins condemned him and he felt helpless. In desperation, he sat down by the window, picked up his Bible and opened it at this verse. 'On reading it,' relates Cowper, 'I received immediately power to believe... I believed and received the peace of the Gospel... My eyes filled with tears... I could only look to heaven in silent fear, overflowing with love and wonder.'[2] What peace — all because God's anger had been turned away from him through Jesus' sacrifice! That is propitiation.

Ebenezer Morris was a powerful preacher of the gospel in Wales early in the nineteenth century. In June 1820, he preached on the text of Romans 3:25 to many thousands of people in the open air. The occasion was the Association of Calvinistic Methodists and the location was the small town of Bala in North Wales. After describing the context of the verse in chapters 1-3 of Romans, he then explained carefully each word in his text. While talking of God's plan to forgive sin through the sacrifice of his Son, Jesus Christ, the preacher shouted out ten times the Welsh equivalent of the word 'propitiation'. The power of the Holy Spirit was upon the preacher. Hearts were melted, people wept and many felt themselves under deep conviction of sin. Soon the huge crowd began to experience indescribable joy sweeping over them like waves of the sea as they saw, many for the first time, that the Lord Jesus by his death had diverted God's wrath from them and suffered it in their stead.

What about you? Do you understand what Jesus Christ did on the cross? Are you able to appreciate that he, and he alone, is the propitiation for our sins?

The context of the verse

We now need to retrace our steps a little in order to explain further the concept of propitiation as it relates to the sacrifice of Jesus Christ. Chapters 1-3 in the epistle to the Romans are crucial for a proper understanding of the term 'propitiation' in Romans 3:25. Let us pause briefly to consider the teaching of these chapters.

The wrath of God is clearly present in the foreground: 'The wrath of God is being revealed from heaven against all the godlessness and wickedness of men' (Rom. 1:18; see also 2:5,8; 3:5; 4:15). This wrath is attributed to God. On God's part, wrath is the necessary reaction of his holy nature against all forms of sin. Without wrath, he would cease to be God. Such wrath is not the impersonal process of cause and effect; it is not a mere natural process. On the contrary, God's personal activity is emphasized repeatedly in the section. Notice, for example, that 'God gave them over' to the pursuit and consequences of their sin. This fact is repeated three times in Romans 1:24,26 and 28.

The wrath of God, then, is personal and is an awful reality. In the remaining part of the chapter, Gentiles are shown to be sinful, guilty and exposed to God's wrath while, in the second chapter, the same facts are established with regard to the Jews. Paul's argument is supported in Romans 3:10-18 by numerous quotations from the Old Testament. The conclusion is undeniable: 'The whole world [is] held accountable to God... There is no difference, for all have sinned and fall short of the glory of God' (Rom. 3:19,22-23).

All people, Jews and Gentiles, are sinners and deserve to be the objects of God's wrath. The good news is that there is one way of escape and this is what the apostle Paul begins to describe from Romans 3:21 onwards. It is the death of Jesus Christ alone which deals with the problem of our sin. By his death, believing sinners are justified; that is, acquitted and pronounced righteous. They are also redeemed, set free from the power of sin, by the blood of Christ. Both terms, 'justified' and 'redemption', are used in verse 24. But the picture is not yet complete. God's wrath still needs to be turned away from us, but the use of the word 'propitiation' in verse 25 completes the picture and solves our problem in a glorious way. How? 'In his blood,' that is, the Lord Jesus in his death bore the full weight of God's wrath — wrath which we deserved because of our sins. His death was a propitiation to God on our behalf. For the Lord Jesus it meant being forsaken by God, unimaginable sorrow, punishment and physical death; for us, it means safety and salvation.

The love of God

The statement in 1 John 4:10 also enriches our understanding of Christ's propitiation on the cross: 'Herein is love, not that we loved God, but that he loved us, and sent his Son to be the propitiation for our sins' (AV). This fact of divine love needs to be stressed in the context of the Lord's propitiatory sacrifice. There is no contradiction at all between wrath and love in God himself. For the love of God is a holy love. God remains holy and just even at Calvary. He did not close his eyes to sin. Nor did he regard sin as being unimportant. There was no slick, easy decision on God's part to forgive sin. His holy nature always hates sin and always, of necessity, responds to punish sin. This is not an arbitrary or vindictive response, but one which is the controlled and inevitable response of his holy nature to sin. Nevertheless, while remaining holy and just, God in his love provided a substitute for us — one who would, on our behalf, bear the divine wrath and punishment due to us. This he did in love.

The initiative was God's, too. 'God presented' (NIV), 'put forward' (RSV) or 'displayed publicly' (NASB) his Son as our propitiation (Rom. 3:25). He thought of it; he devised it in the counsels of the triune God, and he provided it — all because he loved us. His love is the source and reason for Calvary. The point is underscored by the apostle John. God's love of his people, John insists in 1 John 4:10, preceded Calvary. The Lord Jesus was not dying to win the love of God for us, nor was he attempting to coax the Father to help us. Just the opposite was true. Because the Father loved us, 'He sent his Son' into the world. Love planned, prompted and executed the rescue mission of Jesus Christ. The Holy Trinity of divine persons, Father, Son and Holy Spirit, was involved in it from beginning to end.

The apostle John goes even further and reminds us that Calvary was the greatest expression of God's love in history. There has never been such an act of love either before or since. Do you want to know what love is like and what love will do? Then, declares the apostle John, look at Calvary. Are you disillusioned with human love? Has your partner disappointed you? Have you been abandoned, abused or beaten by relatives who should have loved you? Or is your own love to God pitifully weak and compromised? Well, look at the highest, greatest and most wonderful act of love the world has ever witnessed. At Calvary, the Father gave the greatest and most precious gift of all, namely, his own Son. He gave all in giving his only-begotten Son. But that is not all he did. The Father 'spared not his Son, but delivered him up for us all' (Rom. 8:32, AV). He inflicted our punishment on his own Son, and it was to the wrath of an infinite God that the Lord Jesus was delivered on the cross. 'This is love,' declares the apostle John. No one else has ever loved like this.

Conclusion

What then did the Lord Jesus do for us on the cross? He propitiated the Father by enduring in his sufferings and death

the divine wrath in our place. That is what Jesus Christ
achieved, and that is what propitiation means. Remember,
however, that behind and in it all is the vast, immeasurable
love of God. And, 'If we are serious about our Christianity,'
Leon Morris rightly claims, 'we must at least make the effort
to attempt to understand'[3] propitiation.

1. D. Martyn Lloyd-Jones, *Romans: Atonement and Justification,* Banner
of Truth, pp.65-6.
2. Quoted by Elsie Houghton in *Christian Hymn Writers*, Evangelical
Press of Wales, 1982, p.149.
3. Leon Morris, *The Atonement; Its Meaning and Significance,* IVP, 1983,
p.151.

27.
Justification:
not guilty

I am thankful to say I have been to a law court on only a few occasions and then only to accompany, or plead for, someone else who was in trouble with the law. There is one occasion I remember quite vividly. The accused man had been known to me for a couple of years as a respectable, honest person. It was difficult for me to understand why he had behaved out of character on this occasion. The offence committed was not a major one but significant enough for the police to prosecute him in a magistrate's court in Britain. We talked and relaxed together for a while on the morning his case was being heard. When his name was eventually called, we walked into the courtroom. Apart from the court officials, the prosecuting solicitor, a local newspaper reporter and ourselves, it was empty.

After hearing the charge read aloud by the clerk of the court, my friend pleaded guilty. The prosecuting solicitor briefly outlined the details of the case. There was no doubt about his guilt, and he was courageous and honest enough to admit it. He regretted what he had done. No excuses were offered and there was a promise on his part not to do it again. Then, in a brief, moving statement, the young man appealed to the magistrates to exercise mercy and leniency towards him.

It was then my turn to speak. The court naturally wanted to know my position and also my relationship to the man. After providing the information, I proceeded to describe in detail the background and circumstances of the accused person. I had come to know him reasonably well over a two-year period and he had shared both his problems and joys with me. What he had done on this occasion still surprised and saddened me. Perhaps better than anyone else, I knew that a sense of shame and regret characterized his response. Certainly, he was guilty. In concluding my speech, I expressed to the magistrates my willingness to assume full responsibility for the young man in terms of his future behaviour and rehabilitation. If his punishment was a fine, then I would provide the money required to settle the case.

After withdrawing for several minutes to decide their response, the magistrates returned with the verdict. First of all, they reprimanded the guilty man and warned him not to do anything like that again. My offer to accept responsibility for him was gladly accepted. A fine was imposed and this was paid promptly in order to clear the debt. The man was then acquitted. To my knowledge, he has never repeated the offence.

A legal concept

I have related the above incident in order to introduce and illustrate what Jesus Christ did on the cross in justifying sinners. Propitiation involves the concepts of sacrifice and wrath, while redemption has in view the process of freeing slaves. Justification is different again; it speaks of putting us in a right relationship to God and his law, so it draws attention to another important facet of Christ's unique death. In the Bible, justification is often used in a legal setting. The context, therefore, is that of a law court rather than a temple or slave market.

It is our relationship to the law and to God which comes into focus with justification. Are we guilty or righteous before God? Have we kept and honoured all the laws of God? The answer is clear. We have broken God's laws. 'Guilty' is the verdict which the law of God pronounces on us. The penalty for us is death (Rom. 6:23). Romans 5:12-21 shows the results of our sin in condemnation and death for us all. This is precisely where justification comes in, for it speaks of acquittal. The condemned person is declared to be 'not guilty' and righteous. Here is a decision of the judge concerning a person's relationship to the law. To refer to my court illustration again, my friend was guilty, yet after the intervention of another person and the payment of a fine he was discharged. In other words, his relationship to the law was put right again. And that is exactly what Jesus Christ achieved for us in his sacrifice. Because he fulfilled God's law on our behalf and suffered our punishment on the cross, his righteousness is credited to us when we believe personally on the Lord Jesus. The result is that 'There is now no condemnation for those who are in Christ Jesus' (Rom. 8:1). Justification is the opposite of condemnation.

The legal connotation of justification is amply illustrated in the Bible. A helpful classical work on the subject by James Buchanan[1] provides the impressive evidence, as does Leon Morris in his more recent study.[2] The latter establishes that God is seen to work by the method of law and he quotes Jeremiah 8:7:

Even the stork in the sky
    knows her appointed seasons,
and the dove, the swift and the thrush
    observe the time of their migration.
But my people do not know
    the requirements of the Lord.

'Requirements' here translates the plural form of *mishpat*, the word regularly used in Hebrew for 'judgement'. This is a legal term. Morris adds: 'God works by the way of law. Just as he has put into the birds a "law" that covers their migrations, so he has provided laws for his people. In both he is concerned for law.'[3]

When God overwhelmed the Egyptians with plagues in order to release his people, it was as much an act of justice as a work of power (Exod. 7:4; 6:6). Similarly, God's deliverance of Israel is referred to by Deborah as 'the righteous acts of the Lord' (Judg. 5:11). The defeat of the oppressors was a just punishment on the part of God. The prophet Micah, too, used legal language to press home the sin and guilt of his people: 'For the Lord has a case against his people; he is lodging a charge against Israel' (Micah 6:1-2). Or in Isaiah we are told:

> The Lord takes his place in court;
>   he rises to judge the people.
> The Lord enters into judgement
>   against the elders and leaders of his people
>
> (Isa. 3:13-14).

Our duty

Repeatedly, the Old Testament links the law with God. For example, the Hebrew word *'torah'*, meaning 'law' or 'instruction', occurs 220 times and all but seventeen of these instances refer to God's *torah*. Phrases like 'his law', 'my law', 'the law of Jehovah' and 'the law of your God', therefore, occur frequently. What is important to note is that God expects his law to be observed by all human beings. The divine law is binding upon us. As God, he has the absolute right to tell us what to do. All that matters is what God says. He is also the

Creator. We are his creatures who live in his world. Our primary duty is to obey God's laws, which mirror and express his holy nature.

Our problem

This is where our problem lies, and it is a major one. For we have not obeyed the laws of God. We are not right with our Creator and Judge. Nor do we enjoy his favour. In fact, our sins have incurred his wrath and the sentence of death. There seems no hope for us.

This was Martin Luther's problem in the sixteenth century. The young man had everything going for him. His M.A. degree was obtained in 1505 after several years of sustained study. He was doing further studies in law and a promising, lucrative career lay ahead of him. But academic success did not satisfy him, nor was he excited about the prospect of riches and fame. His heart was heavy. The prospect of death, even at a later date, frightened and dismayed him. And he knew the reason why. He was afraid to meet God as Judge. Martin Luther knew that God was holy and also angry towards sinners. His own sin troubled him. 'I was myself more than once driven to the very abyss of despair,' declares Luther, 'so that I wished I had never been created.'[4] There seemed to be no relief for him. One question loomed large in his thoughts: how could he be right with God and win his approval rather than his condemnation? That was his big problem; and it is ours too.

Returning to college one day, Luther was frightened by a thunderstorm and vowed to become a monk if only God spared his life. He was preserved and, within a week or so, kept his promise and entered a monastery. Now he searched for God and salvation more earnestly. Eventually, God showed him through the Bible that Jesus Christ alone had kept the law of

God perfectly on our behalf and also fully suffered the punishment for sinners when he died on the cross. At last, he found
peace with God. Justification was now his.

We can now gather the threads together and mention briefly
three basic aspects of justification in the Bible.

Grace

'It is God who justifies' (Rom. 8:33); here is the uncompromising declaration of the Bible. It is impossible for us to justify
ourselves; in fact, our sins condemn us. David, the writer of
Psalm 143, wrestled with this problem and prayed about it.
'Do not bring your servant into judgement,' he asked God, 'for
no one living is righteous [that is, will be justified] before you'
(v. 2). Like others, David knew he could never attain to God's
standard of obedience. There was no alternative for him but to
seek mercy: 'O Lord, hear my prayer, listen to my cry for
mercy' (v. 1) was his request. Only God could relieve him but
he desperately needed a quick answer (v. 7); he was hopeful
only because of the Lord's 'unfailing love' (v. 8).

To enforce his plea for mercy, David expressed himself in
the language of a court case (v. 2, quoted above). The point he
made is a telling one. David did not want to enter into a court
case against God; the evidence was all against David and he
had no prospect whatever of obtaining a favourable verdict.
And this is true with regard to everyone else. The reason is
obvious: because we are all sinners, it is impossible for any of
us to justify ourselves in the sight of God. How does God
justify sinners then? He does it by grace. Here is the secret.
'Grace' means 'completely undeserved'; it is free, wholly
from God and without any human contribution. We are 'justified freely by his grace ... by Christ Jesus' (Rom. 3:24). The
apostle knew this was true from his own experience: 'I was

once a blasphemer and a persecutor and a violent man... The grace of our Lord was poured out on me abundantly' (1 Tim. 1:13-14). It was the same grace that showed mercy to a swearing, rough drunkard like John Newton. Later, Newton expressed his wonderment in his now-famous hymn: 'Amazing grace, how sweet the sound that saved a wretch like me!' Yes, only God justifies sinners and he does it in grace.

A substitute

Secondly, God justifies by having made Jesus Christ a substitute for sinners. That was happening when Jesus Christ died on the cross. He became our substitute. This is what Martin Luther discovered to his delight when he studied the Psalms of the Old Testament. 'My God, my God, why have you forsaken me?' (Ps. 22:1) was spoken by the Lord from the cross. Luther reflected on these words. What did it mean for him to be deserted by the Father? The utter desolation which, Luther said, he could not endure for more than a tenth of an hour and live had been experienced by Jesus himself as he died. But why? The young Luther now saw the answer clearly. He bore our sins; he identified himself with us and took our punishment. His death then was substitutionary.

Imputation

There is another glorious aspect to justification, namely, that God credits those who believe with the righteousness of Christ. Let me explain. God justifies us by his grace (Rom. 3:24); here is the source of our justification. But we are also 'justified by his blood' (Rom. 5:9). This refers to the ground of justification; it explains how God can 'be just and the one who justifies the man who has faith in Jesus' (Rom. 3:26). His declaration to acquit us must be consistent with the law and holy nature of God. Justice could not be ignored. In justifying us, God does not pretend that we are good, nor does he deny that we are sinners. That would be impossible. What he does rather is to pronounce us righteous with regard to the law and free us from our punishment for having broken his laws. How can he do this? Because he sent his Son to bear our punishment.

It was the thought of God's strict justice which had frightened Martin Luther. 'I stood before God as a sinner troubled in conscience...,' he confessed. 'Then I grasped that the justice of God is that righteousness by which through grace and sheer mercy God justifies us through faith.'[5] God's law required the punishment of sin and the righteousness of obedience. As Luther saw, Christ fulfilled both as our substitute; he obeyed all the demands of the law and paid *all* the law's penalties for us.

That is not all. This 'righteousness of Christ' or, as it is also described, 'the obedience of one' (Rom. 5:17-19), is credited to the believer. Abraham is a well-known example in the Bible (see Gen. 15:6; Rom. 4:3,9,22; Gal. 3:6; James 2:23). Faith has no virtue in itself; faith is rather the grace given to us to rest upon, and receive, the Lord Jesus Christ. As a sinner, Abraham was immediately justified when he believed. At that moment, the Lord imputed to him, or credited him with, the righteousness of Christ.

An illustration of this is seen in Philemon 18. Onesimus, the slave, had stolen from his master Philemon and then fled. On meeting Paul, Onesimus was converted and the apostle urged him to return to his master. Paul wrote a letter urging Philemon to receive Onesimus back, not just as a slave but as a brother in the Lord. Whatever had been stolen, Paul requested that it should be put to his own account and he would settle the debt.

And that is what happened at Calvary. Our sins were reckoned to Christ when he died as our substitute; his righteousness, too, is reckoned to us personally when we believe. Here is justification by faith alone and it takes us to the heart of the gospel.

1. James Buchanan, *The Doctrine of Justification, Banner of Truth,* 1961. See also *Not Guilty,* which is an abridged, easy-to-read edition of Buchanan's work, published by Grace Publications Trust, 1990.
2. Leon Morris, *The Atonement,* IVP, 1983, pp.178-96.
3. *Ibid.,* p.180.
4. Quoted by Roland H. Bainton, *Here I Stand,* Hodder & Stoughton, 1951, p.59.
5. *Ibid.,* p.65.

28.
The substitute

There are, as we saw in the last chapter, several important aspects to the doctrine of justification in the Bible. One such aspect will be developed further in this chapter, namely, that Jesus Christ was made a substitute for us. John Stott uses the arresting title, 'The self-substitution of God',[1] to describe this aspect of Christ's work.

The principle of substitution is well known to us in our contemporary world. In some sports, a player who is not performing well, or who is injured, may be replaced by another player. His replacement is often called a substitute. The substitute functions in the place of, and instead of, the other person. On one occasion I felt myself to be a poor substitute for a professor who should have spoken at a conference. I only went as a substitute at the last minute because the professor had suddenly been taken ill. It was then my responsibility to deliver the main conference addresses instead of the other man.

Other terms, such as surrogate, understudy, stand-in, proxy, deputy, representative and locum can also have the same meaning as that of substitute. An understudy in a drama or opera, for example, functions as a substitute on occasions when the principal actor or singer is indisposed. Or a deputy may go in the place of his superior to an important meeting, whereas a locum works instead of the tired medical practitioner in order to provide him with a well-earned rest. The principle remains the same, namely, that of substitution.

The word substitute means 'in place of'. Here is precisely what happened at Calvary; the Lord Jesus, our substitute, died in our place. God's love and holiness in justifying us were expressed simultaneously by the provision of a divine substitute for sinners. The substitute, of course, was Jesus Christ, who accepted our punishment instead of us.

Substitution, particularly 'penal substitution', affirms James Packer, is 'the basic category' in the New Testament teaching concerning the death of the Lord Jesus. 'The notion which the phrase "penal substitution" expresses,' he adds, 'is that Jesus Christ our Lord, moved by a love that was determined to do everything necessary to save us, endured and exhausted the destructive divine judgment for which we were otherwise inescapably destined and so won us forgiveness, adoption and glory.'[2]

This doctrine of substitution lies at the centre of the gospel itself; it 'cannot in any circumstances be given up', John Stott insists. 'The biblical gospel of atonement is of God satisfying himself by substituting himself for us.'[3]

Substitution in the Old Testament

The work of Jesus Christ as substitute is pictured in various ways in the Old Testament and there are numerous examples of the principle of substitution there. A well-known example occurs in the life of Abraham. God had directed him to sacrifice his only son, Isaac, on a mountain altar. It was not easy for Abraham to obey. However, as he was in the act of obeying the command, God suddenly told him to stop and

Isaac's life was spared. Abraham then 'sacrificed' the ram provided by God 'as a burnt offering instead of his son' (Gen. 22:13). The animal was substituted for Isaac.

In a totally different situation, the local civil leaders were expected to declare their own innocence when there was a murder committed within their boundaries, especially if it was unsolved. They were also required to sacrifice a heifer in the place of the anonymous murderer (Deut. 21:1-9).

It is in the sacrificial system of the Old Testament that the principle of substitution is seen most clearly. R. K. Harrison claims that the book of 'Leviticus teaches that atonement for sin must be by substitution. The sinner must bring an offering which he has acquired at some cost as a substitute for his own life.'[4] Harrison's claim is justified. Having brought his sacrifice, the worshipper then laid his hands on it. This act symbolized his identification with the animal and also the substitution of the animal to die in his place as an atonement for sin (see Lev. 1:4; 16:21-22). When the animal was killed and its blood sprinkled, the worshipper was safe. Here was God's provision for the sinner.

The significance of blood here also underlines the substitutionary nature of the Old Testament sacrifices. Jews were prohibited by God from eating blood for good reason: 'For the life of a creature is in the blood, and I have given it to you to make atonement for yourselves on the altar; it is the blood that makes atonement for one's life' (Lev. 17:11). Not only did the blood sprinkled symbolize the end of physical life, often by violent means, but one person was spared while the animal's life was taken in his or her place; in other words, it was substitutionary. The Passover is another example. Jewish families were spared from death only if a first-born lamb had been sacrificed in their place and its blood sprinkled over their doorposts.

Substitution in the New Testament

The same theme of penal substitution 'is pervasive'[5] in the New Testament as well. Jesus Christ himself made many allusions and references to Isaiah 53, quoting either verses, words, or phrases like 'rejected' (Mark 9:12; Isa. 53:3), 'taken away' (Mark 2:20; Isa. 53:8) and 'numbered with the transgressors' (Luke 22:37; Isa. 53:12). Then there is his silence before judges (Mark 14:61; 15:5; Luke 23:9; John 19:9; Isa. 53:7) and his intercession for transgressors (Luke 23:34; Isa. 53:12). Donald Guthrie concludes that 'There is no doubt that Jesus regarded himself as a substitute in a sense which was reminiscent of, and in fulfilment of, the suffering servant of Isaiah.'[6]

The famous 'ransom-saying' of the Lord in Mark 10:45 is also rich in significance for our theme: 'For even the Son of Man did not come to be served, but to serve, and to give his life as a ransom for many.' Interestingly, the word 'for' translates two Greek words, either *anti* meaning 'instead of' or *hyper* meaning 'on behalf of'. Here our Lord uses *anti,* so the last part of the statement can be translated literally as 'a ransom instead of many'.

There are numerous key verses in other parts of the New Testament which teach that Christ's sacrifice was substitutionary: 'While we were still sinners, Christ died for us' (Rom. 5:8); 'One died for all' (2 Cor. 5:14); 'God made him who had no sin to be sin for us' (2 Cor. 5:21). In the latter statement, 'The concept of substitution is perceived in that he is treated not on the basis of what he is, but what we are. He became our substitute.'[7] The apostle Paul explains in Galatians 3:13 that in order to redeem us from the law's curse, the Lord Jesus became 'a curse for us', that is, he did it in our place.

Another important example is provided by the apostle Peter: 'He himself bore our sins in his body on the tree' (1 Peter

2:24). Notice that the sins are 'ours'; the language used in this verse is substitutionary and the background is probably Leviticus 5:17. Peter's message is clear. James Denney sums it up helpfully: 'Christ took on him the consequences of our sins, he made our responsibilities ... his own. He did so when he went to the cross, that is, in his death... He means that all the responsibilities which are summed up in that death which is the wages of sin, have been taken by Christ upon himself.'[8]

Christ is set forth even more clearly as substitute in 1 Peter 3:18: 'For Christ died for sins once for all, the righteous for the unrighteous, to bring you to God.' The meaning, Guthrie insists, 'is unmistakable — the righteous took the place of the unrighteous.'[9]

Many other references could be cited (eg. Luke 22:19-20; John 11:51-52; Rom. 8:32; 1 Cor. 11:24; 15:3; Eph. 5:2; 1 Tim. 2:6; 1 John 3:16, etc.) but sufficient evidence has already been provided to establish that 'The sufferings of Christ were ... the substitutionary sufferings of the Lamb of God for the sin of the world.'[10]

An illustration

An old Welsh preacher once illustrated the truth of Christ's substitutionary death in a powerful, and now famous, sermon. Towards the end of his message, he pictured a court of law in session. It was a solemn scene. The public gallery was crowded and the atmosphere tense as the judge's verdict was about to be given. In front of the judge stood the prisoner. All the evidence had been submitted establishing the man's guilt. There seemed no hope for the accused. The preacher described the judge putting on a black cap to pronounce the guilty verdict and the sentence of condemnation. He then pictured the law as shouting for the man's death. There were no objections from anyone in the crowded courtroom. The man was obviously guilty and worthy of death.

Just as the prisoner was being led away to his death, there was a loud commotion near the entrance to the court. A man had just come in and wanted to make his way to the front. People stared at him. Others asked, 'Who is he? What does he want?' Eventually, the man turned to the judge and explained, 'I will take the place of the prisoner. Let him go free!' Then the preacher described how the guilty, condemned prisoner was released and the stranger taken as a substitute and put to death.

It is only an illustration and an imaginary story but it serves to explain the principle of substitution. In a far more wonderful way, the Lord Jesus really did become our substitute. This was the only way in which God could be consistent with, and 'satisfy' himself. His holy nature necessitated that sin be dealt with in a proper way. The divine law needed to be honoured. And this meant that the penalty for our sin had to be inflicted. In his love, therefore, he provided a glorious substitute for us.

However, the illustration has its limitations and must not be pressed too far. For example, the Bible does not set the Father and Son over against each other in the work of salvation. True, the Father 'gave the Son' and 'delivered him up' for us and 'made him ... to be sin for us'. But our salvation was planned by the triune God, too. The Father loved us and took the initiative. He provided, inflicted and also accepted the penalty of our sin in the death of his own Son. Here is love indeed — the love of the Father, Son and Holy Spirit. The substitute is none other than God the Son incarnate.

1. J. R. W. Stott, *The Cross of Christ,* IVP, 1989, p.133.
2. J. I. Packer, *What did the Cross Achieve? The Logic of Penal Substitution,* IVP, 1974, p.25.
3. Stott, *The Cross of Christ,* pp.159-60.
4. R. K. Harrison, *Leviticus: An Introduction and Commentary,* IVP, 1980, pp.31-2.

5. Robert Letham, *The Work of Christ*, IVP, 1993, p.134.
6. D. Guthrie, *New Testament Theology*, IVP, 1981, p.448.
7. *New Dictionary of Theology*, IVP, 1988, p.666.
8. James Denney, *The Death of Christ*, Tyndale Press, 1951, p.59.
9. Guthrie, *New Testament Theology*, p.474.
10. Louis Berkhof, *Systematic Theology*, Banner of Truth, 1959, p.376.

29.
Reconciliation

Unlike the words 'propitiation' and 'redemption', the words 'reconcile' and 'reconciliation' are used regularly in conversation and in the media. 'To reconcile' means to bring or restore enemies to friendship; it also means to make peace, make it up, settle differences, restore harmony or, in a well-known phrase, to bury the hatchet. When the enmity has been removed and the quarrel settled, the result is described as 'reconciliation'.

Unfortunately, one area in which reconciliation is often necessary is in families. For example, in England and Wales the number of divorces has doubled since 1971; marriage breakdown is 600% higher than in 1961. A record number of 192,000 divorce petitions were filed in 1990 with 10% of the divorces occurring within two years of marriage. That year, 24.9% of divorces involved people who had been divorced in a previous marriage. Sadly, three-quarters of a million British children have no contact with their fathers following the breakdown of their relationship.

A pioneering family mediation service for Wales was launched some time ago. Family mediation offers parents in the throes of separation and divorce the choice to sit down together to talk and agree about their children. A mediator is present to help them stay calm and focus on the future care of their children. And mediation works; it helps couples reach agreement concerning their children in 70% of cases. Regrettably, parents are often not reconciled and they insist on having a legal separation or divorce. Even royal couples in Britain have had their problems.

Reconciliation also takes place within international relations. The invasion of the Falkland Islands in 1982 by Argentinian troops led to a full-scale military conflict between the United Kingdom and Argentina. It was several years, however, before the British and Argentinian diplomats met for the first time to effect reconciliation. The collapse of Communist regimes in Eastern Europe has led to greater harmony and cooperation between East and West. Reconciliation is taking place.

Another example is the agreement signed between Israel and the Palestine Liberation Organization in September 1993. Palestinians in the Israeli-occupied West Bank and Gaza Strip erupted in joy as they watched television broadcasts showing crowds surging through the streets of the ancient town of Jericho, beating drums and waving their long-banned Palestinian flag. More than 50,000 people poured into the streets of Gaza City, some talking with the Israeli soldiers they had been battling against for years. The agreement was only the beginning of an improved relationship but differences are in the process of being settled while enemies have become friends. All this is involved in reconciliation.

God and man

The above illustrations are helpful in showing us what reconciliation is and why, at times, it is necessary. For all kinds of reasons, people and nations need to be reconciled one to the other. However, there is an even more important relationship where reconciliation is necessary — between man and God. The word 'reconciliation' assumes that a relationship existed between two persons but, having been broken, it needs to be repaired and the two sides reconciled to each other. All this is profoundly true of our relationship to God. An original relationship once existed in which the first humans, Adam and Eve, knew God intimately and loved and obeyed him perfectly. There was no problem in this relationship at all. It was characterized by harmony, peace, intimacy and goodwill. Reconciliation was not necessary.

Suddenly, the situation changed; and it changed dramatically and tragically. We have already seen in chapters 16-20 what happened. Here it is sufficient to say that both Eve and Adam sinned against God. They rebelled and ignored his law. His warnings were disregarded. And the consequences were immediate and disastrous. Fear gripped the hearts of Adam and Eve. Instead of desiring and enjoying fellowship with God, they ran away from him in shame. Both the man and woman made excuses to cover up their sin and attempted to shift the blame onto others. God was angry. First Satan, then Eve and, finally, Adam were all spoken to by God. His words to each were words of judgement and punishment. Adam and Eve were driven out by the Lord God from the Garden of Eden and the divine presence. The harmony had disappeared. Friends had now become enemies. Alienation and enmity were the most prominent features of this broken relationship between God and man.

Alienation

Ever since this major disaster, we have all been alienated from God. This alienation is expressed in two ways. First of all,

from our side there is hostility towards God. We are opposed
to God in our hearts. When his law conflicts with our own
desires then we instinctively go our own way, not God's. Our
instinctive bias is against God. Notice how this fact is repeatedly stated in the Bible: 'We were God's enemies' (Rom.
5:10). 'The sinful mind is hostile to God. It does not submit to
God's law, nor can it do so' (Rom. 8:7). 'The man without the
Spirit does not accept the things that come from the Spirit of
God, for they are foolishness to him, and he cannot understand
them' (1 Cor. 2:14). 'Once you were alienated from God and
were enemies in your minds' (Col. 1:21).

The cause of our hostility and bias is sin. But that is only one
side of the problem. In fact, the other side of the problem is
even more serious. God is alienated from us. And we are told
the reason for this. It is because God is holy; and as the holy
God he is angry with us because of our sin. He is against us
because of our sin (Ps. 1:4-6; 5:4-6; 37:38). Sin arouses God's
hostility; the wrath of God is a reality we dare not ignore (Rom.
1:18; 2:5-8; 5:9-10; 1 Thess. 1:10; 2:16).

Reconciliation, therefore, is the answer to this major problem of enmity and alienation between God and man. The
enmity of God towards us is removed only by the unique
sacrifice of Jesus Christ. He removed the hostility of God by
taking the guilt and punishment of our sin upon himself. But
let me explain this in a little more detail.

The work of God

Firstly, reconciliation is entirely the work of God. This
biblical emphasis must be understood and appreciated: 'All
this is from God, who reconciled us to himself... God was
reconciling the world to himself' (2 Cor. 5:18-19). Notice that
all the emphasis is on God: 'All this is *from God*'; '*God* was

reconciling...' Reconciliation is the work of God. The initiative is God's. He devised and accomplished it. From beginning to end it is God's work and there is no human contribution at all.

The sacrifice of Christ

Secondly, reconciliation was achieved by God, 'through the death of his Son' (Rom. 5:10). While God is the author of reconciliation, Christ is the agent of reconciliation: 'God was in Christ reconciling the world to himself' (2 Cor. 5:19, AV). There is co-operation here between the divine persons in the Holy Trinity. But how did Christ achieve reconciliation for us? Again, we are given the divine answer: 'God made him who had no sin to be sin for us, so that in him we might become the righteousness of God' (2 Cor. 5:21).

In other words, Jesus Christ took our place by suffering the punishment due to us for our sin. Verse 19 gives us some more detail: 'not counting men's sins against them'. God chose not to allow his elect to be punished for their own sin. Instead, he put the guilt of our sin upon Jesus Christ and punished his own Son in our place. By his propitiatory sacrifice, therefore, the Lord Jesus brought the elect out of a relationship of enmity with God into one of peace and friendship. God reconciled us to himself in Jesus Christ (2 Cor. 5:18-19; Eph. 2:16; Col. 1:20-21).

A finished work

Thirdly, reconciliation was accomplished and finished once for all at Calvary when Jesus Christ died in the place of sinners. He did not begin the work of reconciliation and then leave it to be completed by others. For example, while visiting a hospital one day I helped the nurses during a busy period by feeding one of their patients. I managed to do most of the feeding before it was time for me to go somewhere else. A nurse then came to finish what I had partly done. It was not like that at all for Jesus Christ. He finished the work of reconciliation; it was not a gradual work, nor was it a long drawn-out process to which others contributed. Not at all. The use of the verbs in the past tense in 2 Corinthians 5:18,19 and 21 confirms the fact that reconciliation was accomplished and completed in Christ's death. Further confirmation is provided in Colossians 1:19-22: 'For God was pleased ... through him to reconcile to himself all things ... by making peace through his blood, shed on the cross... But now he has reconciled you by Christ's physical body through death...' The language is clear and emphatic: reconciliation was won for us in the sacrifice of Jesus Christ. It is an accomplished fact.

Messengers of reconciliation

Fourthly, the Bible teaches that God has entrusted to Christians the message of reconciliation: 'And he has committed to us the message of reconciliation. We are therefore Christ's ambassadors, as though God were making his appeal through us. We implore you on Christ's behalf: Be reconciled to God' (2 Cor. 5:19-20).

Yes, reconciliation is God's work, achieved and finished in the sacrifice of the Lord Jesus himself. Nevertheless, it is the responsibility of Christians to publicize the news. That is one reason why Christian parents share this good news with their own children. Similarly, a housewife is burdened to tell her neighbours what Christ achieved on the cross and another Christian explains to colleagues at work how they can be reconciled to God in Christ. Some Christian students make an effort on their college campus to tell others the same message of reconciliation and salvation. There are men called specifically by God to proclaim publicly this 'ministry of reconciliation' (2 Cor. 5:18). In their different ways, all these Christians are functioning as messengers of reconciliation. What about you? If you are a Christian are you seeking to share with others the gospel of reconciliation?

Reconciliation must be received

Although accomplished by Jesus Christ in his death and now announced by Christians in various ways, God's work of reconciliation must be accepted and received personally by us. 'We have now received reconciliation,' declares the apostle Paul (Rom. 5:11). You cannot earn it, nor is it automatically given to everyone. No, it must be received as a free gift. 'We implore you on Christ's behalf: Be reconciled to God' (2 Cor. 5:20). You are invited to take advantage of God's grace and the reconciliation achieved by Jesus Christ. All you must do is to believe on the Lord Jesus Christ. By faith, we receive and rest upon the Lord Jesus Christ for salvation (Acts 16:31).

30.
The cross:
specific and effective

I think it ranks as one of the most brilliant rescue operations in modern history. It was certainly remarkable and exciting. I am referring to the rescue of Jewish hostages by Israeli troops in Entebbe during July 1976. Seven armed terrorists boarded Air France flight 139 at Athens on the 27 June; the aircraft had just arrived from Tel Aviv. Once the plane was in the air, the terrorists forced the captain to land at Benghazi, Libya, for refuelling and then to fly the four-hour journey to Entebbe, the capital of Uganda. At Entebbe, they released two groups of non-Israeli passengers and kept seventy-seven Israelis as hostages. Demands were then made for Palestinian prisoners in Israel and in European prisons to be released, otherwise the hostages would be killed. No government conceded to their demands and the situation appeared bleak for the hostages.

Their rescue was discussed at various levels by the Israeli government. All kinds of experts and military personnel were consulted. Eventually, the Air Force believed it could fly 1,200 men and equipment the 2,000 miles to Uganda, rescue all the Israeli hostages and return to Israel safely. After receiving these reassurances, the Israeli government authorized the rescue. Four large Hercules and two Boeing 707s were used. The rescue was completed successfully on 4 July 1976 and the Israeli hostages were safe again.

For the purpose of this chapter, I am drawing attention to the purpose of the Israeli government in organizing this rescue operation. Out of the 246 passengers on Flight 139, Israel had a special interest in the seventy-seven Israelis who were being kept as hostages and whose lives were threatened. They were not indifferent to the needs and welfare of other passengers, but their purpose was more specific and limited. It was to rescue only the Israeli hostages. Israel certainly had sufficient ingenuity and resources to have achieved much more, especially against a weak Ugandan army. However, that was not their purpose. Only one thing mattered, and that was the rescue of the Israeli hostages. After all, these hostages belonged to Israel. Their own people were in danger and concern was felt especially for them. The plan worked, too. All the Israeli hostages were located and safely taken back to Ben Gurion Airport in Israel.

What was the scope of Christ's rescue mission?

The illustration raises questions concerning the scope and purpose of the Entebbe rescue mission. Similar questions need to be asked now concerning the scope of the Lord's sacrifice on the cross. In other words, for whom did Jesus Christ die? How many people benefit from his death? Did he atone for the sins of all people everywhere, or only for a restricted group? These questions are extremely important. They cannot be evaded. One reason is that it is important to know from the Bible the correct answers. Again, the answers to these questions affect our understanding of what the Lord did in dying for us. The subject itself and its implications are of crucial importance. For some, there may be doubts and fears as to whether the Lord Jesus died for them at all. Can they benefit from Calvary or are they excluded?

A word of warning, however, is appropriate before pro-ceeding. Christians do not always agree in their answers to these questions; on occasions their discussion of the subject is marked by ill-feeling and unkind words. This is sad. My desire here is to explain briefly what the Bible says on the subject; I do not seek to be argumentative or harsh; my concern is truth.

The Bible answer can be expressed in six related ways.

Electing love

First of all, God's purposes are always accomplished. Not once has God failed to do what he planned and desired. The point is crucial and has far-reaching implications for the theme of this chapter.

If, in God's purposes, for example, Jesus Christ died for everyone without exception, then obviously the divine pur-pose has failed to a large extent. Just consider, for example, how few Christians there are compared with the total world population. Can God really fail so badly in such an important purpose? Surely not. By contrast, the Bible places the purpose and scope of Christ's death in the context of God's electing love.

Before the world was created, God sovereignly chose those he would save (Eph. 1:4; 2 Thess. 2:13). Are you surprised? Well, God has the absolute right to do as he pleases. And he is under no obligation to save anyone. He is like the potter who chooses what to make from the clay. He is perfectly entitled to choose some people to be Christians and others to be 'the objects of his wrath' (Rom. 9:10-22).

God's choice of his people is unconditional. In other words, he did not choose people because of good qualities in them; nor did he choose them because they would be willing to believe on Christ in the future. It was simply God's good pleasure to choose and save some people. There is no other explanation. 'I will have mercy on whom I will have mercy... It does not, therefore, depend on man's desire or effort, but on God's mercy... God has mercy on whom he wants to have mercy' (Rom. 9:15,16,18).

Having chosen a people in Christ from eternity, in love the Father sent the Lord Jesus into the world to save them by laying down his life for their sins. The Lord's death was, therefore, restricted in scope and intention to the elect of God.

A specific intent

Secondly, there are numerous references in the Bible to the fact that the Lord Jesus died for a specific, limited group of people.

In Isaiah 53, for example, we are informed that 'For the transgression of my people he was stricken... My righteous servant will justify many... For he bore the sin of many' (vv. 8,11,12). The language is specific and restrictive. Jesus Christ did not die in intent for everyone but rather for the 'many' who are also called 'my people'.

A similar emphasis was made by the Lord Jesus himself when he says he gave 'his life as a ransom for many' (Mark 10:45). At the Last Supper he said, 'This is my blood of the covenant, which is poured out for many' (Mark 14:24). The task of Jesus Christ was to 'save his people from their sins' (Matt. 1:21). For whom did he die? Unambiguously, the apostle Paul states: 'Christ loved the church and gave himself up for her' (Eph. 5:25). Again notice here how the scope of the Lord's sacrifice is restricted. Christ did not die for everyone; rather, he died specifically for the church.

This restriction is also seen clearly in Romans 8:31-39. Two important statements here refer to Christ's death: 'He

who did not spare his own Son, but gave him up for us all...'
(v. 32); 'Christ Jesus, who died — more than that, who was
raised to life...' (v. 34). It is the context of these two statements
which makes explicit the scope of the Lord's death. 'If God is
for us,' asks the apostle Paul, 'who can be against us?' (v. 31).
The identity of the 'us' and the 'all' in verse 32 is revealed in
verses 28-30, namely, those whom God foreknew and predes-
tined. The same people are further described in verse 33 as
'those whom God has chosen'. It is for these specifically that
the Lord Jesus Christ died.

Did Christ secure salvation or only make it possible?

Thirdly, the nature of the Lord's sacrifice involves a restriction
in its design. For example, did Jesus Christ die to save everyone? If so, the divine intention has not been realized, for not all
are saved. Consequently some Christians modify the doctrine
by maintaining that Christ died only to make salvation *possible* for all. There are many biblical objections to this theory.
The Bible always speaks in the most emphatic terms of Jesus
Christ securing salvation for his people, not merely making
salvation possible.

Consider, for example, the following words: '... having
obtained eternal redemption...' (Heb. 9:12). Christ did not
merely place us in 'a redeemable position. It means that Christ
purchased and procured redemption. This is the triumphant
note of the New Testament whenever it plays on the redemp-
tive chord,' writes John Murray.[1] Similarly, the Lord Jesus did
not die just 'to make God reconcilable'. Rather, his death
secured our reconciliation (see Rev. 5:9; Titus 2:14; Heb. 1:3;
Rom. 5:6-10). The nature and success of the Lord's sacrifice
are at stake here. This point can be highlighted in another way.
If Christ died only to make salvation possible, then the last

word lies with people, not God. It is the response of people in faith and repentance that makes the cross effective; all depends on the attitude of people. 'The suffering of Christ on the cross,' argues Robert Letham, would then merely be 'contingent and provisional.'[2] And that is not what the Bible teaches.

Christ's prayer in John 17

Fourthly, in addition to dying for us, the Lord Jesus also prayed for us. Notice, however, that he prayed very specifically for a certain group of people: 'I pray for them [that is, the elect; those given to him by the Father]. I am not praying for the world, but for those you have given me, for they are yours' (John 17:9). His prayer here is restricted. He does not pray for everyone in the world, but only for his own people, that is, those chosen by the Father and entrusted by the Father to the Lord Jesus to die for and save. Remember, too, that he was only a few hours away from his crucifixion when he prayed this prayer. His sufferings and death were uppermost in his mind, yet his prayer was restricted to the elect. James Packer asks, 'Is it conceivable that he would decline to pray for any whom he intended to die for?'[3] The Lord's intercession here assumes and implies that his death was restricted in design and effectiveness to the elect only.

The Holy Trinity

Fifthly, the trinitarian aspect of salvation also points clearly to Jesus Christ dying for the elect. The Holy Trinity of persons, namely, the Father, Son and Holy Spirit, were in perfect harmony in planning, accomplishing and applying salvation. God the Father chose the ones to be saved (Eph. 1:4; Rom.

9:10-16; John 6:37-40; 17:2,6,9-10). God the Son then died for those chosen, while God the Holy Spirit applies and makes effective this salvation in the personal lives of the elect. There is perfect harmony within the Holy Trinity. The insistence that Jesus Christ only made salvation possible or provisional by his death 'threatens to tear apart the Holy Trinity. It introduces disorder into the doctrine of God.'⁴

The covenant

Sixthly, the biblical teaching concerning the covenant also points inevitably to the Lord dying for the elect. In an earlier chapter we saw how Adam was made our federal head and representative. Adam was our head also in the sense that organically we were related to him and have descended from him. Jesus Christ, too, is the federal head and representative of the elect. He is the second Adam, whose death was undertaken on our behalf as our representative. Because of our union with Christ, we also died in Christ (see Rom. 6:3-11; 2 Cor. 5:14,15; Eph. 2:4-7; Col. 3:3) and rose with him. This union of Christ with his people is jeopardized and even broken if he does not die for a specific group of people. In dying for the elect, however, he ensures their union with him and an effective salvation. More will be said about this in the next chapter.

Conclusion

No doubt there are questions in your mind and maybe even objections. The subject is important and it is necessary to continue our study of it in the next chapter. Perhaps some of your questions and objections will be answered there. But a word of challenge to you. Believe and understand what the

Bible teaches on the subject. Put sentiment to one side. Do not be governed by what people say. Rather, look at the subject from God's side.

1. John Murray, *Redemption: Accomplished and Applied,* Banner of Truth, 1961, p.63.
2. Robert Letham, *The Work of Christ,* IVP, 1993, p.230.
3. J. I. Packer, *Concise Theology,* IVP, 1993, p.138.
4. Letham, *The Work of Christ,* p.237.

Section V
The cross and you

31.
The cross:
salvation secured and applied

At the beginning of the previous chapter, I referred to the rescue of hostages from Entebbe airport. You may remember that the plan of the Israeli government was restricted to the rescue of seventy-seven Israeli hostages. This was the design and intent of that successful rescue mission.

In a similar but far more wonderful way, God restricted his rescue of sinners to the elect, that is, those whom the Father himself had chosen to be saved. It was for the elect, therefore, that the Lord Jesus died in order to redeem and save them.

Another point of comparison needs to be noted. The Israelis had the ability and resources to extend the scope of their mission in Entebbe, if they had so wished. Their ingenuity and resources were certainly not exhausted by the plan to rescue seventy-seven hostages. More was possible but the plan was wisely restricted. This also needs to be emphasized with regard to the mission of the Lord Jesus Christ. He was the representative, substitute and sin-bearer of the elect. This was the specific purpose decided upon by the triune God. By his life and death, the Lord Jesus fully satisfied all the demands of divine law and justice for those he represented. He died, 'the righteous for the unrighteous' (1 Peter 3:18). A full atonement was made for all the sins of the elect. In other words, the Lord's sacrifice of himself was more than adequate for the whole church.

One can go further. If God's purpose had been to save everyone in the world then Christ's sacrifice would still have been sufficient. His work has infinite value and efficacy. The fact that he is the infinite, glorious Son of God gives infinite worth to what Jesus Christ did on behalf of sinners. There is no defect in his sacrifice, nor is there any diminishing of its value and sufficiency, whether applied to the elect or universally to all. No limit can be placed on the value of Christ's death because he was 'the Lord of glory' (1 Cor. 2:8) and 'the author of life' (Acts 3:15). However, although Christ's sacrifice was infinitely rich in value and capable of saving everyone, God was pleased to restrict the purpose and extent of it to the elect. Make no mistake about it: however strange it may seem to you, it was the purpose of God that the Lord Jesus should die specifically for the elect.

What about 'God so loved the world'?

It is necessary to consider briefly some objections to this teaching. For example, what about the message of John 3:16: 'For God so loved the world that he gave his one and only Son, that whoever believes in him shall not perish but have eternal life'? Is there a contradiction here of the teaching that the Lord Jesus died only for the elect? After all, God 'loved the world' and the invitation is extended to anyone, for the word 'whoever' is used.

Here are some observations which may help to clarify the message of John 3:16. In the first place, the word 'world' serves here to emphasize the universality of God's love. He did not love people in the Middle East alone, or only those in Europe and Asia. The staggering truth is that God loves people from all countries and continents. His purposes are international. The word 'world' sometimes indicates that 'the Old Testament particularism belongs to the past, and made way for New Testament universalism.'[1]

Secondly, the word has a number of different meanings in Scripture (see, for example, Luke 2:1; John 1:10; Acts 11:28; 19:27; 24:5; Rom. 1:8; Col 1:6). When it is applied to people, 'world' does not always refer to everyone (John 7:4; 12:19; 14:22; 18:20; etc.). For example, as used in Romans 11:12 and 15, the word clearly excludes Israel.

Thirdly, the emphasis in John 3:16 falls on the quality of God's love: 'For God *so loved…*' The amazing fact is that God has loved in such a way, and loved people from all parts of the world who are so sinful, guilty and condemned.

An invitation to all

The word 'whoever' is important, too. There is a general and universal invitation which God sincerely extends to everyone through the preaching of the gospel. No one is excluded from this universal invitation. Irrespective of background, status, nationality, religion or behaviour, everyone is invited to trust in the Lord Jesus Christ for salvation. He is willing to receive all who come to him: 'Whoever comes to me I will never drive away,' Jesus Christ tells us reassuringly (John 6:37).

This point was made powerfully early last century by John Elias, the famous Welsh preacher belonging to the Calvinistic Methodists. He was preaching on the text, 'Look, the Lamb of God, who takes away the sin of the world' (John 1:29). During the sermon, he used the phrase, 'The family is too small for the Lamb.' He proceeded to ask:

What is all this travelling from North Wales to South Wales and from South Wales to North Wales? 'The family is too small for the Lamb.' Why all the agitation

these days to send missionaries to the dark millions of
India, to the black pagan of Africa... 'The family is too
small for the Lamb.' Why have you come here today (it
may be asked), to attract people from their duties in the
middle of their working day at a busy time like this? 'The
family is too small for the Lamb.' People! The feast is on
the table; it has been prepared by God Himself; there is
a welcome, there is a call to you all to come; I have come
here today on purpose to announce that there is room for
you at the table; the family is too small for the Lamb.'[2]

All are welcome; the invitation is to all, 'whoever' will come.

What do 'all' and 'the whole world' mean?

Other biblical texts and phrases may be quoted by some to
express their objection to the restricted scope of the atonement. 'Does not the Bible say that Christ "died for all"?' (see
2 Cor. 5:15). Two comments are pertinent here. First, in the
context of 2 Corinthians 5:15 and elsewhere there is an
inseparable unity between Christ's death and resurrection.
Secondly, the statement at the end of verse 15 provides the
answer to our question. He died and rose again for 'all' those
who live for him and who do not selfishly please themselves.
   Or what of the statement in 1 Timothy 2:4: '... God our
Saviour, who wants all men to be saved and to come to a
knowledge of the truth'? Here again the context is important
and helps to determine the meaning of the words. In this
passage the apostle Paul is concerned for all kinds of people
and urges prayer for rulers. Peace and order in society, rather
than anarchy and war, are great blessings which also contribute helpfully to the life and work of churches. The church's
ministry must not be hindered by disturbances and conflict

within society. And there are good reasons for this: God wants all people to be saved (v. 4); there is only one mediator (v. 5), who gave himself as a ransom for all men (v. 6), that is, people from all sections of society and all countries. Prayer should then be offered 'for everyone' (vv. 1,8). The teaching here does not contradict the fact that Jesus Christ died specifically for the elect — the point is that the elect come from different groups within society.

2 Peter 3:9 needs to be mentioned briefly too: 'He is patient with you, not wanting anyone to perish, but everyone to come to repentance.' How does this statement relate to the claim that the Lord Jesus died specifically for the elect? Dr Martyn Lloyd-Jones acknowledged that 'This is a difficult statement … theologically, and it has led to much argument and disputation … it is generally one of those stock quotations which are always brought forward whenever people are discussing election and predestination. But,' he adds, 'to look at it in that way is rather to miss the point which Peter is making.'[3] And he is right.

The point that Peter is making is that God's long-suffering, or patience, partly explains the apparent delay in the return of the Lord Jesus to the world. In this context Peter is answering sceptics who claimed that the Lord's return was unlikely to occur. After all, they affirmed, the earth has not changed in any significant way since creation (v. 4). But they were wrong. Peter first corrects them by showing that a universal flood had taken place early in the earth's history (vv. 5-6). The one who had intervened to display his power and grace in that situation will certainly ensure the glorious appearing of Christ and the end of the world.

In verses 8 and 9, Peter's answer is developed further. God is above time, for he is eternal and he is not governed by the time process: 'With the Lord a day is like a thousand years, and a thousand years are like a day.' Furthermore, God's promise is reliable and 'He is patient with you...' This helps us to understand the apparent delay in the return of the Lord Jesus. God does not 'wish' that any should perish. He has no delight in the punishment of unbelievers; therefore, he delays the end of the world and final judgement. The principle is well illustrated in the Old Testament. A period of 120 years elapsed before God sent the Flood and during this long period Noah preached repentance to his contemporaries. God could have destroyed the people immediately but chose not to do so. Why? Because of God's patience and compassion. 'God always warns before he strikes,' observes Lloyd-Jones, 'and if you read your Old Testament history again from this stand-point, it will amaze you more and more to notice the extraor-dinary patience of God.'[4]

Notice, too, the words, 'with you' or 'toward us' (NKJV) in verse 9. Peter's use of plural pronouns in 2 Peter is significant. The first person plural pronouns ('we' and 'us') refer to Peter and fellow believers who are among the elect (e.g 1:1,2) while the second person plural pronouns ('you') are used of all who read the letter, whether believers or not (e.g 1:4,5). In chapter 2, the third person plural pronouns ('they', 'them') refer to false teachers. 2 Peter 3:9 can now be properly understood: 'He is patient with you' or 'towards us' (the elect), 'not wanting anyone [the elect] to perish, but everyone [all the elect] to come to repentance'. God is patient for the sake of the elect.

Another Bible verse also needs to be considered: 'And he is the propitiation for our sins, and not for ours only but also for ... the whole world' (1 John 2:2, AV). How are we to understand the phrase, 'the whole world'? One point being stressed is that in terms of its efficacy and design the sacrifice of Jesus Christ extends to all generations and countries. His sacrifice was not just for Jews, but for the Gentiles in all the countries of the world. Nor was Christ's death confined in terms of its effect and purpose to the first century; it avails for sinners in all generations. Another point stressed here is that the Lord's sacrifice is exclusive. No one else and no other method or religion anywhere in the world can deal with our sin problem. Jesus Christ is the only Saviour.

The only way

This point needs to be underlined in our contemporary situation, where religious pluralism and universalism are the vogue. Consider an illustration used by Wesley Ariarajah, director of the Dialogue sub-unit of the World Council of Churches, to deny the exclusive and unique atonement of the Lord Jesus Christ. Ariarajah describes an occasion when his young daughter told him that he was the best father in the world. At first, he was pleased to receive the compliment. On reflection, however, he felt that his daughter's compliment was subjective and biased. After all, she only knew one father, even though there might well be many better fathers in the world. Ariarajah then likens this to Christians who claim that Jesus Christ is the best or only Saviour in the world. Having been brought up in a 'Christian' culture and not knowing about other world religious leaders, a Christian can make 'exaggerated claims' for Jesus Christ!

Are our claims that Christ is the only Saviour exaggerated? Certainly not. What does the Bible say?

> Jesus answered, 'I am the way and the truth and the life. No one comes to the Father except through me' (John 14:6).
> Salvation is found in no one else, for there is no other name under heaven given to men by which we must be saved (Acts 4:12).

For there is one God and one mediator between God
and men, the man Christ Jesus (1 Tim. 2:5).

Jesus Christ is not one of many ways to God. He is the only
way. His sacrifice is the only sacrifice for sin throughout the
'whole world'. It is this truth which is being emphasized in 1 John
2:2 and in other references in the Bible which speak of 'the
whole world'.

Those for whom Christ died must be saved

During the last century, Charles H. Spurgeon exercised a
powerful preaching ministry in England. He delighted in
preaching the gospel, but he was in no doubt concerning the
design of redemption: 'We hold that Christ, when he died, had
an object in view, and that object will most assuredly, and
beyond a doubt, be accomplished... Christ came into this
world with the intention of saving "a multitude which no man
can number"; and we believe that as the result of this, every
person for whom he died must, beyond the shadow of a doubt,
be cleansed from sin, and stand, washed in blood, before the
Father's throne.'[5]

Christ did not die merely to make salvation possible for us.
No, he died in order to secure salvation for the elect. Here is
an effective, not a provisional, atonement. Behind the cross, as
we saw in the last chapter, is the electing love of the Father; he
chose a vast number of people to be saved. An eternal,
unbreakable covenant of grace was established by God with
his elect. This covenant was sealed by the blood of Christ when
he procured our salvation (Heb. 9:15; Matt. 26:27-28). In
God's time, the Holy Spirit is sent to each of the elect to give
new birth and bring them to faith in Christ. The Holy Spirit also
indwells them to conform them slowly to the likeness of Christ

and prepare them for heaven. Nothing and no one will prevent or spoil this effective application of the atonement to the elect.

Let Spurgeon have the final word: 'Christ so died that he infallibly secured the salvation of a multitude that no man can number, who through Christ's death not only may be saved, but are saved, must be saved, and cannot by any possibility run the hazard of being anything but saved.'[6] And that is what the Bible teaches. The sacrifice of Jesus Christ is effective as well as specific in its design.

1. Louis Berkhof, *Systematic Theology,* Banner of Truth, 1958, p.396.
2. Quoted by R. Tudur Jones in *John Elias: Prince Amongst Preachers,* Evangelical Library of Wales, 1974, pp.29-30.
3. D. Martyn Lloyd-Jones, *Expository Sermons on 2 Peter,* Banner of Truth, 1983, p.181.
4. *Ibid.,* p.182
5. C. H. Spurgeon, 'For Whom Christ Died,' *Banner of Truth,* 5th issue, April 1957, pp.32-3.
6. *Ibid.*

32.
A glorious harvest

March 1993 was a tragic month for two sets of parents in Warrington in the north of England. One afternoon, the parents were shopping in a busy precinct in the town when, suddenly, an IRA bomb exploded injuring several people and killing two boys, one from each family. Nearly nine months later the United Kingdom government reported that it had been in contact with the IRA terrorist organization responsible for the planting of the Warrington bomb. How did the parents of the two dead boys respond? They backed government efforts to find peace through contacts with the IRA. Colin Parry, who lost his twelve-year-old son, Tim, in the bombing, thought the contacts were 'inevitable'. 'I have said consistently since my son died,' he added, 'I wanted there to be a change. I don't want my son to have died in vain.'

Or think of a very different illustration. 'If one result of Catherine's dying should be that many girls and boys should be saved to live both physically and spiritually, there could well be eternal gain through our loss.' Those were the words of Rev. George Duncan (a well-known Keswick speaker over the years) when he established the Catherine Duncan Memorial Fund in memory of his wife who died in 1985. Gifts received for the fund have been placed in a trust to support deprived children in Calcutta.

The good news is that Jesus not only died for our sins, but he also rose again from the dead, and he now rules the universe and applies all the benefits of his death and salvation to the elect. Tim Parry may or may not have died in vain, but Jesus Christ certainly did not, for many people have been, and are still being, saved through his sacrifice on the cross. His obedience, sufferings and death have turned to our eternal gain. For this reason alone, it was a gloriously fruitful death.

A grain of wheat

This is precisely what the Lord Jesus Christ himself taught: 'Unless a grain of wheat falls to the ground and dies, it remains only a single seed. But if it dies, it produces many seeds' (John 12:24). He spoke these words only two or three days before his death. It was in this context that Jesus Christ spoke about a grain of wheat being placed in the soil and producing a harvest. This picture of a grain of wheat emphasizes the necessity of the Lord's death: 'Unless a grain of wheat falls into the ground and dies, it remains only a single seed.' To help and save us, it was necessary for him to die as our substitute. There was no other way.

The harvest

Notice, however, that the Lord Jesus also draws attention to the harvest which will result from his death: 'But if it dies, it produces many seeds' ('bears much fruit,' NASB). In other words, many people will become Christians as a result of his sacrificial death. And that has happened. Within days of the risen Christ returning to heaven, the Holy Spirit came down in power upon the disciples and Peter was enabled to preach the gospel of Christ with exceptional power (Acts 2:14-39).

Through this one sermon alone, 3,000 people became Christians (Acts 2:41). And that was only the beginning. Every day significant numbers of people were converted (Acts 2:47). Within a few weeks, about 5,000 men had come to personal faith in Christ. For years, the number of Christians 'increased rapidly' (Acts 6:7) in Jerusalem, as well as in other cities and countries. The Lord's claim to build his church in the world (Matt. 16:18) has been honoured.

Since the end of the New Testament period, church growth has not always been spectacular. There have been setbacks and in some countries the church has faced intense persecution. Nevertheless, the church continues to grow as we approach the beginning of the twenty-first century. For example, at present approximately 20,000 people in Africa and 67,000 people in Asia become Christians each day. In addition, while 150 new churches are started each day in Africa, as many as 1,600 new churches are planted each week worldwide. In Korea, twenty-five per cent of the population are said to be born-again believers and members of Protestant churches there. Considerable growth is taking place especially in the Third World. In Latin America, there were only about 50,000 Protestant Christians in 1900. By 1950, this figure had jumped to over five million then to over twenty million in 1970 and fifty million in 1990. Protestant Christians are increasing at three times the rate of the population in Latin America and the number could be as high as 137 million by the year 2,000.

This rich harvest proves beyond all doubt that the Lord Jesus did not die in vain. And an even greater harvest is expected in the future. God promises that many of the Jews will be saved (Rom. 11:12-26) and that a greater number of Gentiles will also turn to Christ before he returns in glory at the end of the world. The Lord Jesus has already reaped a rich harvest and there is still the promise of more to come.

The harvest has been purchased

Make no mistake about it, this harvest was purchased by Jesus Christ on the cross. He made a full atonement for all the sins of the elect; they are redeemed by his sacrifice. This redemption guarantees the working of the Holy Spirit in their lives. They will be born again, brought into living fellowship with Christ, justified, adopted as children into God's family and sanctified, and will reach heaven safely. It is in virtue of the redemption purchased and the atonement made by Christ for their sins that the Holy Spirit is sent to them individually. Christ's redemption removed all barriers and established fellowship between heaven and earth. Through the ransom of the blood of Christ, the elect will all be saved from sin and all its consequences and will be brought into everlasting glory (John 6:39-40; Rom. 8:28-30). A certain, glorious harvest is guaranteed by the redemption Christ purchased for us.

This salvation is guaranteed

There is another aspect to all this. God always succeeds in his plans. He has never once failed. Having chosen to save a people and having given Christ to redeem them, he will see that they are brought by the Holy Spirit to trust in the Lord Jesus. They will reach heaven safely (John 10:27-29) and God makes sure of it. Think about it for a moment. Despite the ravages of sin, the Holy Spirit works a miraculous inward change in a person's life. The new birth takes place (John 3:3-8), sin's grip over that individual is broken and the person will never be the same again. Nor can this person lose his or her salvation. And the reasons for this are numerous. For one thing, God never changes his mind with regard to his choice of the elect. Neither does his love vary. The Lord's propitiation is sufficient, too and his prayers for the elect in heaven are effective. In addition, the Holy Spirit lives permanently within each Christian to strengthen and also make him or her more like the Lord Jesus Christ. Despite the temptations of Satan, the allurements of the world and even the liveliness of sin in their lives, God's people are kept by his power through faith until they enter heaven (1 Peter 1:3-6). Nothing and no one can separate them from the love of God in Christ (Rom. 8:39).

To put it briefly, Jesus Christ did not die to make salvation possible; rather, he died to purchase actual salvation for the elect. And it is the triune God who guarantees that all the elect are brought by the new birth and conversion to trust in the Lord Jesus Christ. Heaven is their destiny and, in God's time, each one will arrive safely. That is guaranteed!

33.
A personal challenge

One of my favourite missionary biographies is the life of Fred
Mitchell entitled, *Climbing on Track*.[1] Not that it is a classic,
or even on a par with the stories of more famous missionaries
like William Carey and Hudson Taylor. Nevertheless, it spoke
powerfully to me. I can still recall its impact and challenge. I
was a young Christian undergraduate when I first read the book
and one thing stood out for me, and that was Mitchell's appreci-
ation of the death of Jesus Christ. Here are some of the details.

Do we need to be saved?

As a fifteen-year-old boy, Fred lived in a village outside
Huddersfield in the north of England. He worked as a trainee
chemist in Huddersfield. One day a mill-worker in the village
named Mr Crapper handed Fred and his friend, Walter, a printed leaflet with the title, *You must be born again*. At the same
time he asked them a personal question, 'Are you saved?'
    Although they both attended the local Methodist Church
with their families, the words were new and strange to Fred
and Walter. They read the leaflet many times over the next
days without understanding its message. 'Why do we need to
be saved? We are active members in the Methodist Church. Is

this not enough? We have never been bad. So what do we need to be saved from?' These were the questions they posed. Dissatisfied with their answers, they decided to discuss the matter further with the man who had given them the leaflet.

'Bearing our sin'

Early one evening, the boys went to a row of narrow, three-storied houses and knocked on Mr Crapper's door. Mr Crapper, who was aged about thirty-five, a kind man and an earnest Christian, welcomed the boys into his home. Hearing of their bewilderment, he prayed briefly before pointing them to several important verses in the Bible. In order, the verses were: Genesis 6:5; Isaiah 64:6; Romans 3:23; Isaiah 53:6; Romans 4:24-25; 2 Corinthians 5:21 and 2 Peter 3:9. They now began to understand and, as they did so, a sense of sin and guilt overwhelmed them. The sacrifice of Jesus was now important to them.

As they were leaving the house, Walter asked a final question, 'Mr Crapper, we cannot understand that scripture, "My God, My God, why hast Thou forsaken me?" What does it mean?'[2] It was a basic question. Moved to tears, the mill-worker explained: 'He was forsaken because he was bearing our sin — *our sin*. God cannot look on iniquity.' With these words, Fred immediately understood the way of salvation and trusted in the Lord Jesus Christ. Later, he reflected: 'It was as if a blind had been drawn up in my soul. The light streamed in. I was saved and knew it...!'[3]

Welcome!

That was Fred Mitchell's response. What about yourself? You are also invited to go to Jesus Christ in personal faith. He promises to welcome you (Matt. 11:28; John 6:37). All you must do is trust in the Lord Jesus Christ (see Acts 16:31).

He is Lord

Perhaps you are already a Christian. Well, a parting word to you as well: if Jesus Christ is your Saviour, he must also be the Lord and boss of your life. This is what C. T. Studd expressed in 1913 at an important period in his life: 'If Jesus Christ be God and died for me, then no sacrifice can be too great for me to make for him.'[4] And that is scriptural (Rom. 12:1; Phil. 1:21). What about you? It is impossible to be saved without living under Christ's lordship.

1. Written by Phyllis Thompson and published in 1953 by the former China Inland Mission, now the Overseas Missionary Fellowship.
2. *Ibid.,* p.20.
3. *Ibid.*
4. Norman P Grubb, *C. T. Studd: Cricketer and Pioneer,* Lutterworth, 1956, p.141.